Martine McCutcheon

Behind the scenes: a personal diary

HarperCollins*Entertainment*
An Imprint of HarperCollins*Publishers*
77–85 Fulham Palace Road,
Hammersmith, London W6 8JB

www.harpercollins.co.uk

Published by HarperCollins*Entertainment* 2003
9 8 7 6 5 4 3 2 1

The Author asserts the moral right to
be identified as the author of this work

A catalogue record for this book
is available from the British Library

ISBN 0 00 716097 6

Set in Futura Light

Printed and bound in Great Britain by Scotprint

Picture Credits
HarperCollins*Publishers* would like to thank the following for providing photographs
and for permission to reproduce copyright material.

p.10 Martine at the Olivier Awards © PA News

p.16–19 Martine in *My Fair Lady* © PA News

p.52 Martine & Julian MacDonald, *Vogue* shoot.
Anders Overgaard © *Vogue*/The Condè Nast Publication Ltd

p.75–77 Martine in *Love Actually*. Copyright 2002 Universal Studios.
Photographer: Peter Mountain

p.110 Martine on *The Frank Skinner Show* © Ellis O'Brien/*The Frank Skinner
Show*

p.112–116 Martine's TV Special. Pictures courtesy of Carlton Television

p.120 Martine in Harrods at the launch of her album *Musicality* © PA News

p.152 Martine at the British Book Awards © PA News

Jacket/Page Design: **'ome**design

Contents

Ever since I was eighteen I've lived my life under the gaze of the press and the public. Everything from my latest career move to my romances, my health and my outfits has been talked about in the papers. It doesn't tell the whole story, of course, and half-truths are something I've learned to deal with, but it can be hurtful to see how the facts get distorted.

I'd lost a lot of self-confidence after appearing in *My Fair Lady* so I decided to take a break from the business. A couple of months later, reading through the diary I kept at the time, I realised just how different the real story of my life was from the version that had appeared in the press. My diary had plenty of sad moments but it was also very inspirational at times. Believe it or not, I actually put it down feeling happy and proud of myself – the strongest of people would have found it extremely tough to get through such a difficult time. It was then I decided I would start keeping my own account, in words and photos, of everything that happened to me – one that I knew I could honestly identify with.

I've always loved photography. I believe that words simply can't capture a moment in its purest form as a photograph can. These days, of course, many photos are airbrushed, especially those of celebrities. And who can really blame us? Why should we show our imperfections when there are plenty of other people to do that for us? But the fact is, none of us are perfect – trust me, I've met them all!

After flicking through many a celeb's photo book, I have to say they're all much of a muchness. Thousands of women write to me about their love life, their weight and countless other things, and usually they're judging themselves harshly in comparison to these images that just aren't real. Of course it's fun to look like a supermodel sometimes, so we've included the odd photograph like that in the book, but mainly I wanted to present a more accurate image, reveal something more honest. You can call me brave – or maybe just plain silly – and I'm not flying a flag for anyone in particular or taking responsibility for making the world a better place, but I hope

Introduction

My philosophy is:
Every day is
a new day.

anyone reading this book will appreciate its honesty and realise that to be true to yourself is what counts.

Several publishers got in touch with me when they heard what I was planning, but I can honestly say that I was sceptical at first about sharing my account with the public. Then I thought, why not? I'm going to have to deal with the press version for the next year anyway! This isn't something I've done because I have an issue with the press, by the way. At times they've been very supportive – they've kept my profile high, which has led to many wonderful opportunities, and I'm very grateful for that. No, first and foremost I did this for myself. But secondly, it's for anyone who is interested in what has happened to me in the last eventful year.

My thanks go to the following people who helped me to put together this picture-led diary of the past year's events: to all my friends and family who allowed me access into their private and personal lives – thanks so much for your understanding and generosity; to Mum, who helped me keep notes on events and helped put together the text of this book; to my publishers, HarperCollins, through all the trials and tribulations that go into producing a book of this kind; to all at Kodak and their never-ending supply of films and throwaway cameras; and to my photographer and great friend McVirn Etienne – you're a real talent.

Extra thanks to the following: Linzi Boyd and all at Surgery PR; Antony Read for being a top PA – now you're an agent, go get 'em!; Richard Curtis, Emma Freud and everybody who was so kind to me on the set of *Love Actually*, with extra special thanks to the press department for letting me use some studio shots; Julien MacDonald; Anna Bingman; Jonathan Malone; Lino Antonella, Daniel Senior and all at Daniel Galvin; Linda Meredith; Moira and Babs at MBC; Rhian Williams at Schillings; Jaine Brent at JJB Creative; Laura Holman; Carl Chapman at Claridges; John and Barry in Spain; Dale Winton; Dee Murran; Eydie and Steve Conn; Hayley and Irene and all the Smiths; Peter and Paula Triplett thanks for all the Paola couture shoes; Jeff Thacker; Paul and Connor at ICM; Laurence Gurlis; Nigel Wright; Simon Lee; Glenda Fraser; Rosemary; Sara Spa; all the Tanners with extra special thanks for this year, especially to James, the love of my life, you're simply the best!; my gorgeous brother LJ, Auntie Kim, Carrine, Howard and baby Lewis; my stepdad Alan, for all the lifts in the car and for making me laugh; Angie and all at Gina Shoes, Marco Pierre White and all at The Belvedere; Nicky and Leslie Clarke; The Chelsea Club and The Lanesborough for treating me like a princess. And finally, to everyone I've forgotten, huge apologies!

In January 2001, a dream I'd long cherished had finally become reality. I'd auditioned for Trevor Nunn and Cameron Mackintosh, and was thrilled when I won the coveted role of Eliza Doolittle in the new stage production of *My Fair Lady*. Rehearsals soon began in earnest, and I spent lots of time perfecting the accent and reading up on the original story, *Pygmalion* by George Bernard Shaw. Those months were tough, but it was a great cast and we all pulled together to make it a wonderful show.

  My Fair Lady is one of the longest stage shows to perform in. At three-and-a-half hours on stage – sometimes seven in one day – it can take its toll even if you're in peak condition. So, as you can imagine, eight shows a week was physically very hard. The singing alone was tough enough – the notes I had to reach night after night would put a strain on any voice. I knew there was an extra weight on my shoulders, too. First I'd been a soap actress, then I'd gone on to achieve success as a pop star, and now I was saying I could make it on stage. Of course I had Trevor's and Cameron's full support, but it was me up there every night trying to prove myself.

My Fair Lady

In hindsight, I shouldn't have believed those who told me that eight shows a week was the norm for a performance of that length, in such a vocally demanding part. As it turns out, some people only do six shows a week, and that's for a six-month contract. My contract was for eighteen months! God, if only I knew what I'd let myself in for.

Still, rehearsals had begun well and, after a few weeks, some members of the cast and some of the musicians started to comment that I had a 'higher soprano' range and maybe I should try a couple of songs in a different key. I'd known from when I was young that I was a soprano – I'd even started to train classically with a private tutor while I was at the Italia Conti Academy of Theatre Arts, and at only 12 years old I loved it – but to be told I was now a higher soprano was amazing and I found it great fun to investigate just how high I could sing. In the end it was decided that 'I Could Have Danced All Night' would sound better if we moved it up a tone. Now that was great, but what we all failed to realise was that while my voice had been used to singing soprano on occasion, it wasn't used to singing higher soprano for three months non-stop and then in a show eight times a week.

The other main difficulty was trying to find a balance between the classical singing and the gritty realism of the acting – both made very different demands on my voice. My music team were totally supportive and I knew it was vital to warm up every night before the show, but then in the opening act I had to scream and shout like a true Cockney! If I'd done most of the speeches as the flower girl 'on voice' or used my voice correctly the whole time, I wouldn't have been completely real or true to the part, and that was vital to me and Trevor – so I tried to combine the two.

During rehearsals I prepared for the role as thoroughly as possible. I knew I had to watch my weight to make sure I looked the part in a role established by the likes of Julie Andrews and Audrey Hepburn. So no pressure there then! And a virus had begun striking down some members of the cast – though I seemed to be fending it off. I'd been very healthy since a bout of glandular fever many years before. But all that was about to change.

Just before the opening night at the National Theatre, I started feeling unwell. I'd already missed one preview, so a voice doctor I'd been recommended to see gave me some steroids specially imported from France. I'd spent years trying to avoid antibiotics and steroids so I was very distressed now that I might need them in order to perform on stage. And of course I felt a twinge of panic – I was gutted that this should have happened on a night that was so very important to me – but I wasn't going to be beaten by a bloody bug! I dug deep and rallied myself to prepare for the biggest night of my career. I absolutely had to get on that stage. I'd worked so damn hard, I wasn't going to let anything stop me.

Playing Eliza in *My Fair Lady*. I get such mixed feelings about this time: amazing highs and dreadful lows, but still an unforgettable experience. Here I am after being transformed into a lady. With me is Mark Umbers who played love-struck Freddie in the show.

In the interval at Drury Lane, before Eliza makes her entrance at the ball, with ladies of the ensemble. We are all on honey and lemon, trying to keep our voices well-tuned.

The opening night coincided with my mum's birthday and it was also the anniversary of the original opening that starred Rex Harrison and Julie Andrews. I felt the omens were good. There was a star-studded audience and the critics were there in their droves. This was going to be my night!

It was a nerve-wracking time and I didn't feel completely well but as I walked on stage that night, I was sure my performance would be one hundred per cent. I knew I'd done my homework, I just had to allow my natural instincts to lead me through it, let myself go and enjoy it – and most of all, be believable as an actress. That was all I could ask of myself. And I'll never forget the standing ovations and the flowers, and the joy I felt after the curtain came down.

It was Trevor who had inspired me most. I so wanted to please him – just for him to be proud of my performance would have been enough – so when he came over to me with a huge smile and a hug and told me the performance was 'breathtaking', I was walking on air. I went through the motions of the after-show party, said hello to everyone and then went off with my family and friends to Sheeky's, a favourite restaurant of mine in the West End. It was a night to remember.

Even so, the critics were still on my mind. But when the reviews came out, I was the darling of the West End. I had achieved my dream. The critics loved me. I was on cloud nine.

But physically I felt shattered. So much had gone into that role already and now I had to face giving the same performance night after night. Most important of all, it had to be the same perfection that I'd achieved that first night. Second best simply wouldn't be good enough, the public deserved the very best.

I never realised just how much pressure I was putting myself under. The West End brigade I worked with advised me to pace myself and hold back sometimes, just to give myself a chance, but I couldn't. Night after night, day after day I pushed myself. I sometimes felt as if I'd been running a marathon with no finishing tape. I was sinking fast. And the non-stop medication for my voice, along with the lack of medication for the virus, was beginning to take its toll.

One sunny Saturday afternoon a few months after the show opened, I lay on my

16.

Eliza goes back to her roots in Act II of *My Fair Lady*. We ended up having to change the hat as it kept knocking the dancers out in one of the dance numbers.

sofa feeling like death, my head was aching and nothing I took seemed to be making me feel any better. My mother had said she was on her way. Meanwhile the doctor had called to see me and he'd told me I had the same virus as everyone else. By the time Mum arrived, though, she knew it was something worse. Call it a mother's intuition, but she said she wanted a second opinion.

Dr Laurence Gerlis, the company doctor, arrived. An ambulance was called and I was admitted to intensive care. At first they were afraid I had meningitis. Steve, my boyfriend at the time, stayed with me overnight, while Mum went home to get some sleep ready to take over the day shift. I stayed in hospital for eight days and they gave me all sorts of tests. Finally a brain scan revealed that there was a clot on my skull that hadn't healed, and that was the cause of the terrible headaches. The virus was all over my body – my throat in particular had been seriously affected – and a large thrombosis the size of a golf ball had formed at the back of my knee. I had bruises all over and I felt truly scared.

The press had a field day. According to the papers, I'd abandoned the theatre and the show and left a seventeen-year-old to hold the fort. That only made me feel worse. I was thrilled that my young understudy had been given the chance to perform, but I desperately wanted to go back. Everything I did at the time was criticised, so let me put the record straight: I never drank any alcohol during my run in the show and only ever went out to eat dinner on one occasion while I was out of the show, after I knew I was returning to work on the following Monday and the show had given me clearance.

It's never easy watching your life unfold in the press, especially when what's written isn't very accurate. I spent many days and nights coming to terms with the fact that my life had been turned upside down due to my illness. I was beginning to think I would never be well again. During the run of *My Fair Lady*, I'd tried everything possible to stay well and fulfil my commitment to the show. It was very hard to accept that now I was home in bed each night, while someone else was getting the applause.

Eventually I returned to the show and started to enjoy it again, but I was constantly nervous that my voice would go or my throat would start hurting again. And worse was to come. My relationship with Steve had been under terrible strain and eventually we broke up. We'd first met playing brother and sister on the TV series *The Knock*. We both had partners at the time, but we met again the following year, single, and very attracted to each other.

Steve was a lovely man who was fiercely protective of his privacy. He'd had a taste of fame after starring in the critically acclaimed *This Life* but he never wanted the media attention – it made him very

What was my relationship like with Jonathan Pryce? This pictures says it all!

uncomfortable. It was something he put to one side because he'd fallen in love with me, but ultimately the non-stop attention of the press was one of the main reasons we parted. We were both exhausted. I was either seeing doctors or vocal specialists or finishing the show at 11pm every night, and then he had to go to Leeds one day to preview a play he was in. I knew as he left that it was over. And I was right – but it was yet another blow to me at a time when I was feeling very fragile.

My voice was deteriorating and, worst of all, my nerve – the thing I could always rely on – was gone. I just couldn't face going on stage any more. I was terrified my voice would go altogether, and I was relying on prescribed drugs to keep me on stage every night. The dream was most definitely over for me. But everyone else seemed to think I was coping brilliantly. I felt embarrassed to talk about how serious my problems had become. Why couldn't I just be confident and well again?

Trevor Nunn had enormous faith in me and I absolutely adored him. I asked if I could go for dinner with him somewhere private, in order to ask him for his help. Like me, he has a genuine passion for his job – in fact it's not our job, it's our life. And now mine was falling apart, bit by bit. I felt that no one seemed to understand I had no choice about my health, that mind had no power over matter. I was coughing up blood, and no amount of dedication could have got me through another five months. I'd now been involved with the show for nearly a year and I needed to be honest about my capabilities for the sake of everyone involved. I felt it was only right that the cast should know what had happened – that I wouldn't be able to continue with the role.

Trevor kept asking what he could do to help me make it work. Unfortunately, even he could offer no magic cure. Despite what's been written in the press, I'll always admire and respect Trevor and Cameron, and we all tried to do what was best. Yes, we had our words, but ultimately I know I tried my utmost, one hundred per cent. Anyone who knows me knows I hate to quit!

At that stage I felt I wanted to end it all, my depression was so bad. That's quite a revelation, I know, but it happens to be true. My friends and family knew how much my career meant to me. They wanted to help me but they didn't know how, while I wanted just one person to give me permission to put myself first, to say that my life came before my career. Like most performers I have an unhealthy desire to please people. If they're happy with me then that must mean I'm doing something worthwhile. Ridiculous, isn't it? Yet, right then, I didn't seem to be making anyone happy or pleasing any of my critics, even though I was trying so hard.

What was also frustrating me was that there were many times I was on stage – a lot actually! But the press would still say I was away and that people who'd paid a

Myself and Dennis Waterman thank our conductor for a great opening night at the National Theatre – we were all on cloud nine. An unforgettable moment.

fortune for tickets were going to miss out. That made me angriest of all. But, whether I liked it or not, I had to admit to my current situation. I had to finally put myself first and leave the show.

By January 2002 I was at my lowest ebb ever. My friends tried to drag me out and about to the local clubs in Chelsea, get me to let my hair down and have fun again. Full of sadness though I was, surprisingly I had lots of offers from the opposite sex at that time, varying from dates to full-blown relationships. But I was numb, I had little faith in anything any more. A relationship was the last thing on my mind. However, I did meet James Tanner, a lovely man who was to become a valuable and trusted friend. He made sure I had fun, no matter what. I'd met him through a mutual friend in a club and after meeting him a few more times I knew he would be good for me. When I met his family I realised why he was such a brilliant person. They have a great love of life and it was just what I needed.

But right then I had no relationship, no career and no future, so I decided to go away and think things through, try to see where my life was going. Barbados has always been a place for me to relax and unwind, so it seemed to be the natural place for me to go. My Auntie Kim came with me – she's my mum's younger sister, she loves to travel and she's always loads of fun – along with a girlfriend, Octavia, and my business manager, Richard. Mum flew out two days later, but she arrived feeling very unwell herself. By now the virus had hit her too and she was feeling under stress as she was so worried about me.

Going to see my voice doctor for the fifth time, in Summer 2001. He told me I wouldn't be able to go on stage without steroids.

I returned to Britain to face another barrage of bad press. I'd had no choice but to quit *My Fair Lady*, but no one seemed to care how much I'd lost. 'Sick Note', 'My Fat Lady', 'Eliza Do-Little', 'Martine the Dumped Lady', were just a few of the comments I had to endure, and none of them was true.

I felt like quitting the whole business, becoming an ordinary girl and finding out what life might have in store. I needed to stand back from the situation, so I decided to go to Spain and talk to my trusted friends, John and Barry.

John and Barry are a wonderful couple. I met them years ago at their house in Marbella through a mutual friend. They're so wise and they always give me their honest opinion. Accompanied by my best friend, Linzi, I went to stay with John and Barry, and I talked while they listened. They advised me that I wouldn't just be able to leave the business behind me. Anyway, something big would eventually come along. They made me really think about my life and the opportunities that might come my way. Basically, John and Barry gave me hope.

What I needed most of all was time to get a healthier perspective on things, to rebuild my shattered confidence. And, God, I have! I've learnt an awful lot about myself. Knowledge is power, as they say, and now I have the tools to protect myself in the future. I knew I couldn't allow myself to go back to those dark times but, in order to carry on, I needed to be more in control. I would never let anything – no matter what or who – make me feel so inadequate again, because nothing is worth it.

The main thing that lifted my spirits was my
Olivier Award win.

On the night I won my Olivier Award with, from left to right, Auntie Kim, my friend Dee, Mum and Linzi.

Later, on the night of the Olivier Awards, at Brown's nightclub where Callum Best and friend enjoyed the party. We danced the night away and everyone was thrilled for me.

It took me months to get my head around all this, of course. I couldn't expect to learn so much overnight. But by May 2002 I truly felt like my old self again. The main thing that lifted my spirits was my Olivier Award win. I'll never forget the feeling of dread as I was getting ready to leave my flat in Kensington that night. My stylist Anna Bingman could sense my nerves and she was totally positive and complimentary about how I looked and what I'd achieved. But no one, not even my agent, truly thought I would win it – not because it wasn't deserved, but purely because of all the press and politics. Sod them all, I thought. I may not win but, God help me, I'll be the most talked-about loser for a long time. After all, being in a soap, having a number-one record and now having more press for a musical debut than anyone I know doesn't exactly keep you out of the papers, does it?

I also decided that I'd be the best-dressed loser ever! I wore a beautiful Collette Dinnigan top. It was backless apart from jewelled straps and had a gorgeous sequinned butterfly on the front, and I teamed it with Gucci tailored flares and some pretty diamonds. I felt wonderful – despite being scared of the ceremony and bumping into many of the cast I had now left in *My Fair Lady*. I sat down with my agent, said my hellos, was ignored by the ever-gracious Jonathan Pryce (my Professor Higgins in the show) and waited for the Best Actress category to come up. I didn't hear my name properly – it sounded muted, so far away. I put my hands to my face. Oh God, had I heard it right? My agent ended up saying 'It's you! Go on, Martine – it's your award, go get it!'

I was so happy. I made my speech, politely thanking people (some of whom didn't deserve it), explaining how the part had been my passion and how, despite all the hard times, I was convinced it was worth it. Afterwards the paparazzi and press were going crazy for pictures and interviews. I couldn't stop grinning. I was introduced to some of the judges and said I couldn't believe I'd won.

'Why?' they asked.

'Because I thought you'd read the bad press and be put off, me being ill and so on.'

'Martine, we saw you independently four times and every night you were magic. The best. We don't give awards for the fittest person or the longest marathon runner. It was for the best actress. You were the best and so you won. Don't forget it.' And I never have. That night we really celebrated. First the Ivy, then on to Brains and Attica nightclub – and we were chauffeured around all night in a blue Rolls-Royce.

On another night out with friends, in China White's, who should I be introduced to but Liza Minnelli and David Gest? I couldn't believe they were there! I've always been a huge fan of Liza's and of her mother, the late, great Judy Garland. I even ended my debut album, *You Me This*, with 'Maybe This Time', which Liza made famous in *Cabaret*. It's still an all-time favourite of mine to sing.

In the back of a Rolls-Royce at the end of a very long day, after many glasses of champagne. The driver took this – he knew I was doing a photo diary and snapped us. We found it on the film when it was developed!

Liza has always been very open about all her problems, and her instant vulnerability mixed with dry humour and wit appealed to me immediately – and made me adore her. She'd read all the good and bad reports about *My Fair Lady* in the press and she talked to me for hours that evening. I felt absolutely chuffed to meet her that night. She gave me plenty of sound advice – you don't go through all that Liza's gone through and not learn a lot.

We instantly hit it off and exchanged numbers. I really wanted to hear from them again but I thought I'd never be able to ring them. How wrong I was! We stayed in touch for a couple of months, chatting for hours on the phone and meeting at The Lanesborough hotel for tea. When you meet Liza, you can't help but love her, though even I was shocked when she asked if I would be bridesmaid at her and David's wedding. I was delighted but had to ask: 'Are you sure, Liza? You haven't known me for very long!'

'What do you think I am? A sucker?' she laughed and carried on in her American twang, 'You think I don't know a good person when I see one, honey? You're a darling girl and we adore you – I love you like family. I don't know why it's happened so fast, but it has. I would be honoured and so would David if you would accept.'

I said yes. She flung her arms round me and cuddled me tight. 'You are so darling!' And the wedding was unforgettable. Tony Bennett was one of the many singers, Michael Jackson and Liz Taylor were part of the wedding party, and there was me taking it all in. Even the rehearsal was exciting and Liza was hilarious when she ran up to me and said, 'I'm going to have to remove you from the building – you're too young!' Everyone laughed their heads off.

On the big day, I was wearing an amazing couture Valentino outfit and I felt a million dollars. I was spoilt rotten and Liza never forgot about me – she's a sweet, sweet woman and I have nothing but good to say about her.

After the wedding, she came to the Royal Albert Hall to do some gigs and sat me in the front row most nights. I was honoured – it was something her mother used to do with Liza whenever she was nervous before a gig. Sometimes she would look at me throughout a whole song. She's an amazing performer with true star quality.

She gave me a good talking to once, when the press got to me. 'So what? They write all this crap about you and you're gonna let it all end? You're only just beginning, darling. I've had a drink problem, hip replacements, break-ups and I've nearly died – I'm still up here doing my stuff, so get up off your ass and back up on stage where you belong.'

It took me a while – but I did.

I love the month of May. It's my birthday month, and this year I wanted to get right away from London and celebrate with my friends and family. Things were looking up, too. John and Barry had been right – my career was about to move in a new direction.

Richard Curtis is a marvellous man whose talent I really admire and he had a new project in the pipeline. So I was overjoyed when I was asked to audition for a part in the film, which was to be called *Love Actually*. I read for the part of Natalie, a young tea girl who works at 10 Downing Street. And guess who the Prime Minister was? None other than Hugh Grant! When the call came that I'd got the part, I immediately called my mum, who happened to be in the car at the time. Now Mum has a little routine she always follows when news of a success comes my way – she does a tap dance. OK, I admit she can't really tap dance, but it's something she just has to do. So when I called her she made her husband, Alan, stop the car. Then out she jumped, mobile to her ear, and did a little tap dance, right there in the street.

My mum has only ever wanted me to be happy. She's always believed I was destined for show business, even though it was a struggle for her when I was younger and she was doing three jobs a day to keep me in ballet tights and tap shoes. Even when I felt I wanted to leave the business, she let me make the decision. She always supports me, no matter what choices I make.

My 26th birthday in Spain at Villa Tiberia on Marbella's Golden Mile. After *My Fair Lady*, I spent some time thinking hard about what I should do next.

Everyone needs reassurance in this business and we all strive to give one hundred per cent in all that we do. The press can either make you feel great about yourself, or can upset both you and those you love. Just for the record, despite what's been written, Mum is not my manager and never will be. She's happy just being Mum. Although she helps me in many ways, she does it as my mum and not because it's her job.

In addition to news of the Richard Curtis film, for which I was due to start rehearsals later in the summer and filming in October and November, I received news this month that my record company still wanted to make another album with me. Paul Conroy, president of Virgin Records (part of the EMI/Liberty group), had come to see me several times in *My Fair Lady*. He liked musical theatre, although if I remember correctly he couldn't be described as an avid fan. Anyway, it was he who had suggested to Hugh Goldsmith, the head of A&R at Innocent Records (a subsidiary of EMI and Virgin), how fabulous it would be if we could do with an album what Trevor and Cameron had done for musical theatre. In other words, the album would attract a very different audience to the musical genre because of the artist's appeal.

Hugh Goldsmith had come to see the show and an offer was put on the table there and then, while I was still performing on stage surrounded by press hype. I would have had a lot of support from Paul and Hugh if I'd accepted – and the advance was tempting too. Despite all the rumours, I was earning very little while I was in the show. At the time, though, I had enough on my plate. The show was plenty to be dealing with on its own, while we were also recording the original cast album. It was a shame because it would have been perfect timing. But I said up front that I believed the show would suffer if I had a major campaign with yet another musical album.

I love the month of May. It's my birthday month, and this year I wanted to get right away from London and celebrate with my friends and family.

Now, a year later, they were telling me that the album offer still stood. I was a little unsure about it but it was lovely to know there was work in the pipeline. The timing wasn't great even now – being honest, I was only just beginning to feel my voice was right and there was no longer a buzz surrounding *My Fair Lady* – but Paul and Hugh were terrific, they'd been the major keys to my successes with 'Perfect Moment', 'I've Got You', 'Talking In Your Sleep', 'On The Radio', and 'I'm Over You', amongst others.

Whenever I go to Spain, if I don't stay at Barry and John's I like to stay at the Las Dunas in Estepona. It's a lovely hotel where I'm always well looked after, and I have fond memories of every visit. Most of all I enjoy having lunch with my friends and family, sitting by the sea or the pool, or in the open courtyard of the hotel.

I first visited the hotel with Patsy Palmer when I was in *EastEnders*. I'll never forget that particular holiday – not so much for the holiday itself, but because while we were there we heard the news of the death of Princess Diana, someone I respected

and found extremely inspirational. Strangely enough, I'd met James Hewitt in a bar only the night before, and not long before that, I'd been chosen by the readers of the *Daily Mirror* to be pictured wearing one of Diana's dresses on the front page of the paper after they'd successfully bid for it in an auction. I'd been hugely flattered and couldn't wait to meet her, so her death affected me enormously.

This year we held my birthday dinner at the Villa Tiberia, a lovely restaurant in Marbella. Lots of people made it out there and it was a great evening. My cousin Carrine made the trip and, when she arrived, she secretly broke the news to me that she was pregnant. I was thrilled for her but sworn to secrecy. Carrine and I virtually grew up together. Mum and Auntie Kim would arrange days out for us when we were young and we often used to go on daytrips to the seaside. Carrine has since moved to Wales and made her life there, but we're still close.

My mum and Alan also came out to Marbella for my birthday, as did Auntie Kim. Barry and John came along, as well as Dee, Linzi and Sharon, and some other friends from Spain. Dee has been a dear friend for many years since I met her on the waltzers at a premiere with Mick Hucknall. She's always protected me from the pitfalls of fame despite her own wild-child image. I'm pleased to say she is now a very happy, settled mum – but she still has the drive to succeed and, yes, she is still wild!

Linzi and I met through Dee at Teatro's restaurant years ago but it was only around the time of *My Fair Lady* that we became incredibly close. She had her own personal problems and I had mine – we were a right pair! We've helped each other through so much and, looking back, she was one of the few people

Dinner in Puerto Banaus with Jaine Brent, William Folland-Conroy and his partner Christian. It was a time when I needed a lot of support, and they were all there for me. From left to right, Christian, William, Jaine, me, Linzi.

who was truly there for me. I love her like a sister and don't know what I'd ever do without her.

Sharon is the eldest of the group. She is a nutty, bubbly, very pretty Northerner. She knows absolutely all there is to know about health, diets and fashion. She is very organised and the 'mother' to the group, yet she has the best figure out of all of us – cow!

My girlfriends are deeply involved in the industry – Linzi has her own fashion PR company and is now a regular presenter on Fashion TV. Dee was 'Miss Dee', famous for her club nights and connections, and Sharon is a designer for many high-street chains. It's nice that they're all so successful in their own right. They know how tough it is for women these days – and how Sharon and Dee do it with kids, I'll never know.

Mum had organised the flowers for my birthday dinner. There were peach rose petals scattered on the table and a huge bouquet of peach roses in the centre. It was beautiful, a brilliant evening all round. After dinner Mum and Alan, Kim, Carrine, John and Barry all headed off home, but the girlies and I decided to make it a late one and headed off to clubland. We had a real laugh. We weren't allowed into one particular club, as one of our friends was wearing a trendy pair of trainers and the club's dress code is a bit old-fashioned. So two of us pretended they'd just got married, and they let us in! Sometimes it pays to be an actress.

I had another lovely surprise when Jaine Brent, William and his partner Christian all arrived in Spain for a long weekend. I've known Jaine, William and Christian for some time. They're lovely people and great friends, as well as being involved in the business. Jaine runs a very successful branding agency and she matches artists with the right product for endorsement deals. I first worked with her agency years ago in Ireland when they arranged a personal appearance out there for me. Jaine is a fabulous woman, she has a great heart and she's the hardest worker I know. We've done lots of good work together. So, with a new album looming, I decided I would talk to Jaine about the possibility of her looking after me while I worked on it. She would only have a six-month contract, but it would be a hard six months as there would be lots going on. She agreed and we started to arrange meetings back home to get the ball rolling.

The month had been a success. Things were looking up. Maybe the year ahead would be a good one after all. Maybe I could finally put the past behind me and start looking towards the future. I felt better in myself and my confidence was returning. I was beginning to feel that the old Martine was coming back – for the first time in ages I felt strong, ready to face anything. Britain was my home, and I wasn't going to let anything or anyone drive me out.

Sharon Georgio and Tommy Rocket pretending to get married so we could get into a club. Not the prettiest bride I've ever seen.

I returned from Spain, boxing gloves on, ready to face whatever life had in store for me. The summer was on its way and I felt well rested. June is a wonderful month – sunshine, sunshine, sunshine.

My little brother LJ (which stands for Laurence John) was born on 9 June 1991, and on his birthday I always take him out and give him lots of treats. He's very different from me, but despite the fifteen-year age gap we're very close – I call LJ my wise old soul. He comes out with little sayings that you would expect from your grandad, but he always makes sense. He's my best boy.

It would be true to say that LJ loves his food, especially burgers. Now I'm very health conscious, and I like to encourage LJ to eat a variety of healthy food and to drink plenty of water. Who am I kidding? LJ tries very hard to be good when he's with me. On his birthday though, I let him indulge.

I was born in Hackney, in East London, but while Mum was still married to John McCutcheon, LJ's dad, they decided to move to Essex. I got to know Hornchurch and Brentwood very well and we would often go out to eat in local restaurants. LJ, Alan and Mum live in Essex, so naturally we take him out to celebrate in the area. This year we chose Simply Blues, an American burger restaurant in Hornchurch. He invited some of his close pals along with Nanny Hemmings, my natural father's mother, who's as mad as a March hare and always gets the party going. I'm so glad that, despite the fact that my dad isn't in my life, she is. She's wonderful and we all love her to pieces.

June

All smiles as we are greeted with flowers in Singapore – despite the jet lag, we were so excited.

June was a glorious month in many ways. I was given the opportunity to go to Singapore – how fabulous is that? Nicola at *Glamour* magazine called my mum to ask if I would be willing to go courtesy of the magazine and the Singapore Tourist Board. I wanted to take Mum with me but she was too busy helping set up my website. My Auntie Kim jumped at the chance, though, and so did photographer McVirn Etienne (known as Mac), a great friend who I'd asked to help me record my year with his camera. Mac's brilliant as he's able to take care of my security as well!

The first thing you notice as you get off the plane in Singapore is the humidity. We were greeted at the airport by representatives of the Tourist Board and found everything laid on for us. We were treated like royalty. Our hotel, the Hotel Fullerton, was amazing, very grand, and our suite was wonderful. All the staff came out to greet us when we arrived and we were each given a beautiful bouquet of flowers.

An itinerary had been arranged for us and we were kept very busy as there's so much to see and do in Singapore. The view from the hotel swimming pool is one of the most breathtaking I've ever seen. The country itself is an eclectic mix of old traditions, various religions and modern technology. One minute you're looking at an old-fashioned oriental barge hung with little lanterns; then, as you watch its journey, you see it meander through Singaporean cafés, traditional English-style bridges and modern skyscrapers. The weather is a real mixture too. I remember being in the pool one morning, and having the whole place to myself. This wasn't so surprising – I think it was about 5am – but I was jet-lagged. The weather was warm and humid, and the moon was in the sky but the sun was coming up and it felt like it was about to rain. I looked up at one of the skyscrapers and there, at the very top of the building, flashed what I can only describe as red lightning. Meanwhile there were people crossing a brightly lit bridge near the hotel on their way to work, not even looking up. They obviously see things like that every day, but I won't ever forget it.

The country itself is an eclectic mix of old traditions, various religions and modern technology.

What an amazing experience visiting Singapore was. *Glamour* magazine flew me out there through the Singapore Tourist Board. Here I was on my way to consult a traditional Chinese herbalist.

The Singapore Tourist Board had arranged some fantastic things to do on our itinerary. We went to Little India where they made us our own saris. We also went to see a Chinese herbal doctor – another unforgettable experience. They wanted me to boil up some Chinese moths and then drink the liquid. Apparently it's supposed to get your stomach moving, if you know what I mean (though the broth wasn't necessary in the end!). I am, however, a great believer in Traditional Chinese Medicine. After all I've been through, I've investigated every means of keeping myself well and it's definitely something that has helped me. The doctor did make me laugh, though. Apparently she's quite a star in Singapore and she wanted to give me her autograph. She kept saying something that sounded like 'Shirley Bassey', but I still have no idea what she meant!

After that we went for rickshaw rides and tasted some of Singapore's delicacies. The journey was hilarious. None of the rickshaw owners wanted to take Mac – he's built like a tank, while the Singaporeans are so tiny that they looked terrified at the prospect of pedalling him around. They weren't keen on Auntie Kim either as she is very tall and couldn't fit her legs in! Meanwhile I just sat there and roared with laughter.

The food in Singapore is delicious and you can get different types of sushi and Chinese food at very reasonable prices. I was really surprised at how trendy some of the bars and restaurants were. We went to one place called 'Asia' – it was

At the Chinese herbalist. I was given lots of samples after my 'analysis'. Most of what I was given was great but I drew the line at dried moths, which I was told to boil in water and drink.

Right: In Little India market, where you can buy the best sari material or freshly ground spices.

Far Right: Raffles Hotel, one of the most beautiful hotels I've ever been to, with a very glamorous history. It's also where the Singapore Sling was invented.

A wonderful sushi restaurant where the food was great and the views were better. It's a shame I'm terrified of heights.

Bathing in milk and rose petals at a spa with my Aunty Kim. With matching shower caps.

beautifully decorated and the music they played was great while the service was second to none.

Of course, while we were there we also had lots of spa treatments – probably the greatest ever. And the massage, the milk baths and the acupuncture were all divine, darling! The whole trip was fascinating, one of the most interesting I've ever been on. I even sang on the stage of the beautiful new opera house they had just built. In fact no one had sung there yet, so I was honoured to be the very first. I loved my time there but for the first time in ages I really wished I had a man to share it all with. It's funny how really happy times can sometimes make you feel more on your own than sad times. Oh well, what will be will be, I thought. You never know what's around the corner.

Back in the UK, June also provided me with the opportunity to look for venues for my upcoming TV concert. Myself, Jaine and the record company knew it would be difficult to market an album of this kind, so were asked to do a TV special. I couldn't quite see myself singing a musical number on CD:UK!

I originally wanted to film a live musical show at the Royal Albert Hall and at first numerous different TV companies had promised me the earth. But, sadly, none of the promises were fulfilled – there's a surprise! Time was short as these things need to be booked way in advance, but everything seemed to be left to the last

We stayed at the Hotel Fullerton, which has the warmest pool I've ever been in up on its roof – this is where I watched the amazing electrical storm. Back down to earth after the most extraordinary sunset I've ever seen.

The massage, the milk baths and the acupuncture were all divine, darling!

Smug me ...
they have a Tiffany's and a great department store in Singapore.

minute. I decided to visit the set at Pinewood to see what they had to offer. This time I was being promised a Vegas-style show with laser beams and helicopters, but none of that materialised either. Another surprise! I would like to point out that Pinewood were brilliant and none of it was their fault. The studio was an interesting place to visit because the new 007 movie *Die Another Day* was being filmed at the time. Pierce Brosnan was gorgeous and I met him very briefly. Sorry, guys, I tried to get a picture with Halle Berry, but she was too busy filming. Take it from me, though, she is incredible!

People have asked me why I decided to do a musical album. The press weren't sure what to make of the idea, since my career in pop with 'Perfect Moment' and the album *You Me and Us* had been such a success. But I'm a creature who enjoys many different aspects of entertainment, and I love to try everything.

My second album, *Wishing*, included an amazing single, 'I'm Over You', which went straight to number two behind the Spice Girls' last single, and 'On The Radio' is still played in clubs now. *Wishing* sold hundreds of thousands of albums and I was extremely pleased, considering the record company had changed the timetable for the third single. By then I was rehearsing for *My Fair Lady* and couldn't promote it, but while the campaign lasted we did very well.

I do like to be versatile. Being in *My Fair Lady* didn't mean I had abandoned my singing career. I'd been given an amazing opportunity to show that I genuinely could sing live, I'd been offered my dream role and I wasn't going to give up the chance of fulfilling it. But now I was keener than ever to bring out another album.

By this time JJB Creative, Jaine's company, had begun acting as my management. It's a very tough job – everyone wants a piece of an artist and your management has to protect you from all the demands – and to be totally honest, my record label wasn't helping. No studio time had been booked for me to record, and time was running out to find a possible venue. As is usual with these things, finance takes priority and you never get what you're promised. It was around this time that I

Very excited at the prospect of holding my televised concert at Pinewood Studios. We're just about to take a peek at the James Bond set.

Diane Crystal Honey, in charge of sales and marketing at Pinewood, with Jaine and myself. My day there was great fun and we all wanted the concert to happen.

Back in London, after a fashion show at the Royal College of Art, where I was Julien MacDonald's guest. I met up later with Christian at the Wellington Club to carry on a fantastic night.

Hugging Julien in front of a mural outside the Royal College of Art. We clicked from the moment we met and soon became close friends.

realised big changes were happening in my record company. Paul Conroy, the president who had supported me throughout my first two albums, had left. I might be wrong but I had a feeling that my new team at Innocent were less enthusiastic about this latest project, something that made me sad because their support was vital in order to make it a success. However, I was contracted to do a job and I would fulfil it to the best of my ability. I knew it would be tough: I prefer having familiar faces around me who know the way I work and how to get the best out of me, but that didn't happen in making this album. It made it a very difficult time for me. I'd enjoyed working with the same team on both my previous albums and was pleased with the results. Still, I decided to give it my best shot with the team I had left and use my own press company, stylists and make-up artists for the TV special. And I would begin making calls to producers myself, to try and get the ball rolling.

Even at such an early stage Jaine and I were having to fight battles. The filming schedule set by the production team of *Love Actually* had to take precedence, and all my other projects had to fit around that. It was something I was more than happy to do. After all, Working Title, the film company, had shown great faith in me and made it an absolute pleasure to work for them.

It was all new to me but everyone on the film seemed to know exactly what they were doing. I had lots of costume fittings and finally we decided to make my character timelessly chic, but in an accessible way. We stuck with cute ponytails and simple make-up to emphasise her youth. I had great fun on the make-up truck and was in my element with all the fuss. My character is very sweet and self-deprecating and has a softness that I think is irresistible. She was a dream to play – especially opposite Hugh.

In the meantime I'd agreed to put together this book, and I was avidly taking pictures at every opportunity. Mac, my professional photographer, was already on board, and he followed me everywhere. My life was being viewed through a lens once again, but now for the first time it would be from my point of view. To be honest, I was more nervous about fulfilling my obligations to the book than I first anticipated. We all like to have an element of control in our lives and if something goes wrong or we're worried, we can maybe gloss over it or ignore it. I knew this couldn't happen with the book. I also knew that there might be trouble ahead for me and I had no idea how to avoid it. And all of this was to be captured on camera … bloody perfect!

In my profession, nothing ever seems to go at an even pace. It's my fault to some degree, but opportunities and work keep coming along and I just can't ignore such wonderful chances. After all, you only live once. One minute I feel everything has passed me by, and the next I'm running around trying to get things done. When I look in the mirror sometimes and analyse myself I can see that my inability to pace myself is one of my biggest faults. I love my work and I'm a perfectionist to the point of obsession – I have to give my all in everything I do, and if I'm not putting in one hundred per cent I feel I'm cheating the public and myself too. So if people around me don't do the same, I feel like I'm wasting my time as my industry doesn't suffer fools gladly.

I was aware the months ahead would be filled with lots of work. All I needed to do was pace myself and get my team to support me. It sounded easy – but could I pull it off?

At Karen and George's Beauty Centre with their children – they didn't want to hug me as I'd just had a sticky St Tropez treatment!

I really love the summer months, and July turned out to be a very busy one offering some fabulous opportunities – as well as lots of hard work. So no change there then. My album meetings continued through July and I was very busy with little chance to take even a single day off. Nine times out of ten, it isn't my actual job that stresses me out as that takes the least time of all – an afternoon of vocal recording here, a twenty-minute interview there, ten minutes in front of the movie camera . . . that's fine. What takes time is all the meetings to decide the most straightforward things. I've talked to lots of other artists about this and we all laugh about it – it's the same everywhere. One of the most famous sayings in the business is 'Hurry up and wait', and it's very apt. Everyone tells you to get a move on and you mustn't be late, and when you get where you're supposed to be, no one is even ready!

Block Row Seat
A4 20 49
Enter by: RED SIDE
ear Channel Entert Seat
Proudly Row
Block 20 50
A4 20
Enter by: RED SIDE
Clear Channel Entertainment
Proudly Present

ROD STEWART
LIVE 2002
8.00pm
Wednesday 03 July 2002
£42.50 Ticket Presented to Guest
3 1077 030702 171935A

0022521473000000

Me and Rod at Wembley
– he's still one of the best!

By now I was concerned that there still seemed to be little support for my album. The original concept had been that I would perform alongside some other well-known artists, so I tried setting up my own meetings with artists such as Westlife and Blue. I thought it would be great to have them sing on an album like this. It would show off their versatility, bring a younger market to this kind of music – and it would also be fab for my record sales! Blue were on the same label as me, and the boys themselves were really up for the opportunity to show off their voices with something different, but the record company didn't seem keen.

I couldn't understand why they should object. All right, musical theatre and swing jazz bands weren't the music of the moment – but Robbie Williams had recently pulled it off with his best-selling album ever, and that was full of old big-band songs that had gone down a treat. Surely when Blue were lined up for TV appearances with Donny Osmond they weren't just thinking of the modern market. The boys have brilliant voices. They became friends of mine and I heard them singing Sinatra like a dream — and that was just when they were mucking about. It would really have helped me out and would have been so much fun. More importantly, it might have been great for business for the record company. But the company didn't see it like that. I was told that they wanted me to perform as a solo artist.

It's a shame they wanted things that way, but it didn't stop me meeting up with some friends to see what they thought. Jaine (my manager at the time) acts as Blue's branding agent, so I asked her to arrange another meeting with them. I met up with Duncan at Gordon Ramsay's restaurant before popping in to see the rest of the boys in Dartford. It was around about now that, according to press reports, I was romantically linked with Duncan. He's a real sweetheart but, no, we were never boyfriend-girlfriend material.

The boys are brilliant, and I must thank them for their support throughout what was a difficult time for me. Even when they knew they hadn't been granted permission to appear on my album, they would still call me up with some fab ideas and sing Sinatra songs down the phone. I'm thrilled they've done so well. Even if they weren't meant to be on the album, they have had a great year and I hope they do get the chance to show off just how talented they are with their future projects.

This month there were also lots of dress fittings for the film *Love Actually*, and I was bombarded with meetings for the book and album as well as for the film. I also managed to hook up again with the lovely Nicola from *Glamour* magazine. I'd agreed to do a charity photo for the magazine to raise awareness of breast cancer. After the shoot, Nicola and I decided to go and watch Rod Stewart, the best rocker in the world. He's still utterly marvellous, and I thoroughly enjoyed myself. I think it's probably one of the best concerts I've ever been to, although he

The Moschino launch party (I'm wearing Moschino, of course!).

kept apologising for losing his voice. I didn't even notice, I just shouted 'Go on, Rod! I know how you feel but you sound amazing!'

That night I bumped into a friend who took us to the best seats for the second half of the show and we could see Penny, Rod's girlfriend, dancing in the wings to 'Hot Legs'. God, she's got some pins on her! Nicola and I were very envious. My mum was also there with some of her friends, but I didn't even find out 'till I called her afterwards. She was in good spirits and said how much she'd loved it too. I found that concert very inspiring – I could see how relaxed Rod seemed with the whole thing. He was just there to perform and give everyone a great night's entertainment – no more, no less. I decided I should be more like that.

There were so many invites during July that it would have been impossible to go to everything unless you did it for a living. I can sometimes get in the region of forty

At the Givenchy fashion show in Paris. The collection was fabulous and Julien MacDonald had done an amazing job: I was proud of him.

My feet are killing me! Here I was decked out in Givenchy in glamorous Paris, but the shoes had to come off and I made a run for it across the street. Then Mac stopped me for a photo.

In my suite at Hotel Coste
after this fab coat
arrived. I spotted it on a
model who was, of
course, pin thin and fell
in love with it.

invitations a month (depending on how popular I am at the time) ranging from the cool fashion crowd to the elite. You get very different people at the various parties and it's a bugger for the wardrobe – one minute I'm in my trendy gear, the next I'm Yves Saint Laurent-ed up! One group of people is always there though – the paparazzi. These evenings are often fun, but they're hard work. Someone always has their eye on you, whether it's for a photo or an 'exclusive interview' – dishing the dirt, basically.

I was invited to a Moschino opening in Curzon Street, where I was snapped by loads of paparazzi and, shortly after that, I trotted to James Tanner's sister Natalie's thirtieth birthday party in Streatham. One minute I was being photographed at a top London fashion shop, the next I was with my mates in Streatham singing my heart out on their karaoke machine. Well, I've always said that I want to have choices in life, 'To walk with kings nor lose the common touch'.

Ever the optimist, I was looking for the opportunity to take some time off this month and get away to Spain again – I just love Marbella. And where there's a will there's a way. Barry and John always have an open house for me, so when a few spare days came up I grabbed the chance to be with them.

Not very long after I returned, I got the most amazing invitation. Julien MacDonald, a true friend as well as a very talented designer, asked me over to Paris to attend his fashion show. I was so excited. It was one of the most thrilling weekends I've ever spent. I was booked into the gorgeous Hotel Coste and, once I'd settled in, I was invited to the House of Givenchy. I actually went to the place where Audrey Hepburn was fitted, which was a dream come true. It was there they fitted me from head to toe in Givenchy.

Julien made an amazing fuss over me and I was treated like a true princess. I went off to the show feeling a million dollars. During the fashion show, I saw the most amazing coat – Linzi, who was with me for the whole trip and was looking gorgeous herself, agreed it was incredible. I ended up being photographed for *Vogue* magazine wearing that coat. I'd been spotted at the show by one of the writers for the magazine. She was staying at the Hotel Coste too and asked if I would be interested in doing an interview about couture. I agreed, then after I'd gone back to my room and was sprawled out on my beautiful bed the phone rang. I stretched a hand out, happily exhausted with all this glamour, and it was Jane Martin, PR for several labels including Givenchy. She said that *Vogue* had asked if I would like to do a shoot on my own and with Julien – there and then in the hotel! I was so happy. It was one of my dreams come true.

It was an unbelievable thrill. There I was, pictured in *Vogue* with my darling Julien and wearing that beautiful coat. Later that evening we were all whisked off to

Many of Audrey Hepburn's outfits were designed here. I met the seamstresses who still sew the dresses by hand. Julien made me buy the coat and paraded me up and down his studio workshop in it. He loved it too, and we ended up both being photographed for *Vogue* at Hotel Coste. One of my ambitions fulfilled.

That evening, at a big dinner for Givenchy's couture clients. Me and Ivana Trump are discussing investment and property (honest!). Note I still have my favourite coat on.

Being photographed for Vogue
at Hotel Coste.

One of my ambitions fulfilled.

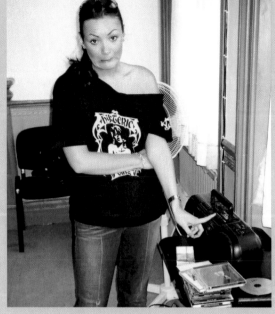

Clockwise, from top left: Recording *Musicality*. I'm not happy, as I'm at the wrong recording studio.

That same day, now at the right studio but with the wrong equipment. I really had the hump and was not in the mood to sing.

I cheered up as we began recording. I wanted to show the record company what I could do, by producing a really good demo.

Listening to a demo vocal of 'The Man Who Got Away', during which I'd hiccuped at a heart-rending moment. The engineers kept playing it back to me ... OK, you had to be there.

dinner where I, Martine McCutcheon, sat and talked about good investments with Ivana Trump. Everyone asked who I was ... a very memorable weekend.

I was soon brought back to reality as the recording studios beckoned. I really felt everything had been left far too late. I must admit I was a little anxious, to say the least. I felt that my record company wasn't getting behind me. Why had they asked me to do another album, I wondered, when they didn't seem that interested? Things got worse. I was due to do some recording work and was sent to the wrong studio. Not just that, but when I arrived at the right place I found that it had no professional equipment – nothing. Surely this wasn't right. Eventually, after numerous calls, I was moved to Metropolis Studios, but I had to organise it all myself. I wasn't happy. I felt that Jaine Brent was my only support, trying her best to liaise with the record company on my behalf. All in all this wasn't a good start to a difficult campaign.

I decided to focus on other business. I needed a PR company to arrange the press coverage for the album, so I met up with Moira Bellas and Barbra Charone at MBC. I loved them instantly; they were totally professional and very approachable. By now things were also picking up on my website, and 'martinesplace.com' was becoming a reality. Good things were starting to happen. I filled Moira in on the difficult circumstances surrounding the album and she seemed really clear on the balance that was needed to market a musical album whilst making the most of my name as the artist.

A year had gone by since the original album offer. While I was thrilled that the deal still stood, in that time a lot of money had been spent on new staff and new artists for EMI, a lot of changes had been made, and I had to accept that I wasn't a priority. Many of the people who had faith in me previously were either involved with new projects or had left altogether. Maybe this album was a farewell gesture and that attitude wasn't going to make it a success. I had committed myself but now wished I hadn't. It was going to take so much time and energy and, ultimately, what for? Maybe I was being negative. Maybe I was wrong. Whatever the case, I would at least try to use it to build my confidence and help me enjoy performing again.

This month I got away from the problems in London by going to Bournemouth with Glyn, my driver, who has a boat there. Dan, my personal trainer, came too. I'm not very good on boats, but I do love a challenge. I should have known that it was a bad idea to go clubbing the night before, but I couldn't resist the opportunity to have a night out with Dan at one of the clubs down there. Duncan from Blue was there, strutting his stuff with his friends (he was brought up near the area and still loves it). Luckily he didn't have to get on the boat the next morning. He took my gang round to several clubs and the free champagne flowed. I was surprised at

56.

I needed to build my confidence and enjoy performing again.

With Jason Hazeley, who helped on this album and was co-writer on my first album *You, Me and Us*. He's an absolute genius. I originally proposed he arrange and produce the album – maybe next time...

just how good a couple of the clubs were – after all, you do get spoilt in London.

Early the next morning, the phone went. It was Dan. 'Hi, babe, Glyn's just called me, he's waiting for us on the boat. Fancy going on the sea and eating his wife's home-made picnic?' Well, you should have seen Dan and me on the boat that day – we were so ill. Never again.

Legal meetings, and lots of them, also took place this month. I don't enjoy them, but they're made bearable by Rhian Williams at my legal firm, Schillings. Rhian is young, attractive and a bloody good lawyer. We get on very well, which helps, and she always has my best interests at heart. There was a particularly difficult issue hanging over our heads which needed sorting. Thankfully the outcome was favourable, and I really must thank her, Simon Smith and Keith Schilling for all their hard work.

July wouldn't have been the same without a trip to the Wellington Club. I always have a good time when I go there – Jake, the owner, and Christian, his son, always look after me very well. The Wellington is in Knightsbridge and I believe it used to be an old pub. They've transformed the place and now it's a restaurant and bar. It's very comfortable and quite exclusive so you don't get lots of people behaving like idiots, you can just switch off and let your hair down. Jake and Christian really spoilt me for my birthday back in May too. They filled the place with roses, laid on rosé champagne and invited about thirty of my friends along, and we had a fantastic evening. Lots of my very normal, down-to-earth friends were pictured by one of the big tabloids as we left, and I had loads of messages to tell me that their families had rung them up, saying things like 'You're a star now! Have you seen yourself in the paper?' I'd forgotten that it isn't actually the norm to see yourself in the press – and it was a reminder that it's good fun sometimes.

The thing that my friends always notice is how much people stare and make comments about me, as if I can't see or hear them! It's almost as if you aren't real, because you are a star. I'm very lucky, though. Thanks to the character of Tiffany and my own journey with the press, the public – both men and women – seem to really like and support me. They see a girl who came from nothing, but made the best of everything she had. I guess it gives people something to aspire to and if I've been an inspiration to just one person, that's a great thing to have achieved. When I'm in a bar or club sometimes I love to have the night to myself – but that's just not a part of the job. Being honest, I do feel safer when I'm in the VIP area of a club: you get fewer bumps and knocks and you can spend some time just relaxing with your friends.

Some people just smile or wave at me, while others hand notes to a friend or security guard to pass on to me. Some just think 'Let her get on with her night'. But

most people come up and say hello and tell me they've loved something I've done – whether it's 'Perfect Moment', *My Fair Lady*, *EastEnders* or a dress they fell in love with and where did I get it? (And that's just the boys!) The vast majority of people are so lovely to me that they often make my day. The odd occasion when people can be rude is when they're drunk, and take offence when you've had enough after ten minutes of them slurring all over you! But this doesn't happen often and I can honestly say I've been very lucky. If anything, people look out for me and are protective, even though they don't really know me. That's something I'm very thankful for – the public are often fascinated by certain celebrities and pop stars but that doesn't necessarily mean people genuinely like or support them. I'm grateful that at the moment they seem to like and support me.

The boys from Blue. We were going to duet on the album but unfortunately it didn't happen.

This month was good fun, but also contained an important opportunity for me … to conquer my fear of singing live. Every year in Wales there is a huge concert called Bryn Terfel's Faenol Festival. I'd been asked to appear with Bryn in his 'Music Under The Stars' night, which goes out live on Radio 2. I must admit I was nervous at the thought of appearing live for the first time since *My Fair Lady* but I knew that, in order to conquer my demons, I needed to do it.

I thought long and hard about appearing at the festival, and I must admit there were times when I thought it was far too soon to appear on stage again. I wasn't yet sure that I had the self-confidence to feel in control on stage that night. Putting it off had given my voice the time it needed to mend, but ultimately I knew the only way to find out if I could do it was to try it – properly, in front of thousands of people. God, I hate my job sometimes!

In the back of my mind, I knew I couldn't put off singing live much longer. I was scared – there was no getting away from it – but this black cloud that hung over me had to be dealt with and the festival seemed to be the perfect opportunity. I've always had a brilliant following in Wales, the people there appreciate a good voice and what it takes to look after it. What's more, there would be limited press, so if I fell on my backside I would be able to cope. I'll do it, I decided.

August

Gŵyl y Faenol Gyda
BRYN TERFEL

25·08·02

Jaine Brent was handling all the festival arrangements and the organisers very kindly let me bring my mum and Alan, who are always on hand to support me. The location was ideal. My cousin Carrine lives in North Wales with her husband Howard, and I knew my Auntie Kim was visiting that weekend too. So, if all went according to plan, the family would be there to see me.

We arrived on Friday, flying into Manchester, and were picked up by two cars. Mum and Alan went with one driver and Jaine and I went with another, called Garem. We checked into the hotel and, after a quick bite and a drink, went straight to the rehearsal rooms. I decided on three numbers: 'The Lady is a Tramp', 'Maybe This Time' and 'Zing Went the Strings'. The rehearsal rooms were magnificent and the sound quality was quite superb. The whole orchestra were present and I felt my confidence start to grow. When the conductor raised his baton and the music begin, I heard my voice come out with ease. I felt at that moment I'd jumped the first hurdle. Jaine, Mum and Alan had been sitting at the back of the room and, seeing their beaming smiles, I knew that I sounded as good as ever. Going through my three numbers, I can honestly say that I felt on top of the world. All too soon, though, the rehearsal was over and we were on our way back to the hotel.

James Tanner, who was becoming dearer to me by the day, spoke to me on the phone that night, and he could hear how terrified I was about my performance the next day. He must have loved me even then, because he drove all the way from London and found his way to the middle of nowhere that night to support me. It was about 2am when he arrived. Better still, he looked incredibly handsome! I couldn't think about all that right then, but little did I know that those feelings weren't going to go away.

When Saturday dawned we were all up early and had a hearty breakfast, although I avoided dairy products as they affect my voice and I had to be very careful. The sun was shining but there had been heavy rain during the night and the festival venue, which is a large field, had become very muddy. Jaine, as usual, didn't have suitable footwear, so Mum decided to make a trip into Bangor with her to buy some trainers. While they went shopping, I pondered over what colour dress to wear.

The dresses had been lent to me by designer Neil Cunningham and they were gorgeous. I had two identical dresses in different colours. Once Mum and Jaine returned, I asked their opinion and we were all unanimous that I should wear the bronze one. The purple dress was beautiful, but the bronze one was more striking and suited the lighting much better.

Carrine, Howard and Auntie Kim arrived in time for lunch. Jaine had called

Not my usual choice
of footware for a
performance but on this
occasion the not-so-lovely
green wellies saved the
day ... and the evening.

In my Winnebago at the Faenol Festival, or 'Bryn Fest', open-air concert in Wales, before performing in front of 10,000 people – a great place to conquer my fear of singing live again. It had rained the night before and everyone was sinking in the mud, so we were all given a complimentary pair of wellies.

In my Winnebago at the Faenol Festival, or 'Bryn Fest', we were all given a complimentary pair of wellies.

Russell Grant, who lives locally, and asked him to join us. It was such fun. Russell is an absolute darling and I was so grateful that he came along. He has a unique calming manner and he made me feel completely at ease. He loves musicals, and I had no hesitation in asking him to join us for rehearsals.

Before we set off, we all had tea on the terrace. It was beautifully sunny and the gardens of the hotel were simply breathtaking. There were walks around the grounds and I particularly liked the herb garden. Each of our rooms had its own little terrace and the views were wonderful. I loved that part of Wales. Unfortunately, I can't speak Welsh, but everyone was very accommodating, and I did try the odd phrase here and there!

It was soon time to leave for the full-on rehearsal. Everyone decided to come down for it and we all made our way with our various drivers. I had my own Winnebago right next to Claire Sweeney. The mud was worse than ever by now and getting to the stage was going to need luck as much as judgement. Eventually a lovely security man came running along holding a pair of green Wellington boots. Yes, they were for me. I sat on the steps of the Winnebago and posed for a picture. Inside, everything had been laid on. It was very comfortable and there was lots of fruit and plenty to drink. I was very well looked after.

When it was my turn to rehearse, Mum made her way round to the front of the stage with Russell, James and Jaine. I was left with Alan and William, who was also there. Alan often acts as my security man, and I always feel safe when I'm with him or William. Today, though, they acted as my bearers and carried me through the mud to the stage.

At the Bryn Fest with Bryn Terfel – a great classical singer – and the lovely Claire Sweeney. I was terrified at this moment as I was on next and everyone else had done so well.

Well, here I was, on stage with the orchestra. I stood there in a tracksuit and Wellingtons, looking silly but feeling great. The music started and off I went. The three numbers went without a hitch, and my confidence soared.

Back in my Winnebago again, I felt elated. I just knew the concert would go well, and Mum and Russell were so excited. They'd been able to visualise the performance from the audience's point of view, and they, too, were sure the night was going to go well. We all went back to the hotel while Russell dashed home armed with everyone's birthdays, as we all wanted our astral charts done!

It was time to relax and get a little rest before the performance. It was going to be a proper concert that night. Bryn Terfel is an amazing singer with a terrific range and incredible stage presence. Ken Bruce would be presenting alongside Bryn, and Paul Bateman would be conducting the BBC Concert Orchestra.

Nothing in my life ever runs smoothly, though, and guess what? When I returned to my Winnebago it was locked and I couldn't get in. And no one seemed to have the keys. The only way in was via Claire Sweeney's Winnebago, which was attached to mine via a connecting door. Having scrambled through I realised that the connecting door was locked as well. My tummy was turning over through nerves by now, as it always does before a performance, and it was having a laxative effect. God, I was nervous that night, and I needed the toilet desperately.

In the end, there was nothing to do but use Claire's – I'm sorry, Claire, it was me that used your loo!

We eventually found a key to open the connecting doors and I managed to get dressed and was ready in the nick of time. I was on last, so I waited in the wings while Bryn and Claire performed. Then it was my turn. I walked on stage to an amazing standing ovation. The Welsh certainly know how to make you feel welcome. I was back, and I performed my three songs to wonderful applause. Mum and James sat with Carrine, Howard and Auntie Kim. As I was singing 'Maybe This Time' Mum and James held hands as I reached the top notes. They both jumped up and led the applause as I finished the song. That's a sweet memory I will keep with me always.

The performance went very quickly, and to finish the evening all the performers came on stage together. I was given a little Welsh dragon and a beautiful bouquet of flowers and the night ended with a spectacular firework display. After the crowds had gone, we made our way to an after-show party where there was a huge barbecue and lots of wine. But we'd done our bit by this time and so we all decided to make our way back to the hotel.

It's hard to describe, but once the performance is over you're still on a massive high. So it was a time for celebration, not for bed. Carrine and Howard stayed

On stage (without wellies) and conquering the fear! It turned out to be one of the best live performances I'd ever done. I knew it would be great as I walked on stage – everyone was on my side. It was a beautiful evening.

with Auntie Kim for a little while and we all decided to play a game. Mum, Jaine and William were already drinking vodka. Usually I like to pace myself, but now I could really relax, so I decided to have a drink too.

We love the 'Post-It' game. What happens is that everyone in the room is secretly nominated as a well-known character, film star or pop star, anyone famous. The name is written on a Post-It note and stuck to your forehead, so you've got no idea who you are, and you have to ask questions to discover your identity. This time we decided that Jaine would be Priscilla Presley. She's terrible at this game – despite the most hilarious clues, she just couldn't guess who she was meant to be. When she was the last one left, Mum decided to give her a clue, so she explained that Jaine was married to the King and then did an Elvis impersonation. 'I know who I am,' Jaine screamed in sheer delight, 'I'm Shirley Bassey!' The night continued in the same vein and everyone had a marvellous time. I went to bed feeling much, much better.

The next day I would be heading home happier than I'd been in a very long while. James had been so wonderful. When I saw him all dressed up at the concert, I'd started getting butterflies in my stomach. He gave me a lift back to London and I kept catching myself staring at him. Whenever I tried to speak, my words kept getting caught – which can be embarrassing when you're stuck on a motorway for hours! After about my fiftieth attempt to say a sentence in English he laughed and asked if I was OK. He looked so bloody sexy. 'Of course – I'm great,' I said. I looked out of the window and thought, 'Could do with giving you a big, gorgeous kiss though!'

I like to see my brother LJ as often as possible, so I decided to give Mum and Alan a break in August and take LJ home with me to spend the night at my place. LJ is a really good lad when it comes to bedtime, but as a treat I decided to take him to the Tanners' for a karaoke night first. He's very shy normally but, once he got on the microphone, he came into himself and we just couldn't get him off. It was great fun and he loved it. He slept very well that night and didn't want to go home the next day. Mum and Alan had a great weekend as well, and for me it was a real pleasure.

Jaine Brent called me later that month to ask if I would like to give out an award at the *GQ* Awards night. I've always been a fan of Gordon Ramsay, and he'd asked if I would give him his award if he won Chef of the Year. He's not only a highly talented chef but also a wonderful man with a fantastic personality. I agreed and decided to wear a beautiful black Armani dress, which was a real head-turner. There were lots of great people there, from David Bowie to Jade Jagger, and one of the nicest men in the business, Ioan Gruffudd – he's best known in England for

My brother LJ, who I love to pieces and spoil rotten, celebrating his debut performance at the karaoke night.

Gordon Ramsay and his wife at the *GQ* Awards on the night I presented him with the Chef of the Year award.

his brilliant leading role in *Hornblower* – won Man of the Year. Naturally Gordon was also there, along with his beautiful wife. He did win the award – and he really deserves it – and I had a great night.

It was around now that I decided I needed a car. I didn't have my own transport and there are times when I like to get into a car and just drive. I discussed all the options with my friends, and Glyn, my driver, suggested getting a classic car. The idea really appealed to me, so off I went to see what was available.

As soon as I entered the showroom, I knew I'd found the car for me. There she was, all lovely and shiny and a beautiful blue colour. She was a classic 1970 Mercedes Sports soft-top and I named her Bonnie Blue. The name was originally used in *Gone with the Wind*, a classic film that I love, and it really suited this gorgeous little car. There was nothing better than driving around with the top down, the car getting lots of admiring glances and compliments. I was so proud of her. It didn't take long for the press to picture me with her in the papers. What made me laugh was that, because Glyn was with me, they thought he was my latest fella!

Classic cars need love and attention, and despite all my efforts, Bonnie soon decided she was knackered and didn't want to start, never mind go anywhere.

She may have been beautiful but, for the next couple of months, she was a right pain in the backside! Finally I decided she had to go up for adoption – I think I will stick with my gorgeous Range Rover in future.

Rehearsals for the film *Love Actually* started in earnest this month. I found it all a bit daunting, I must admit. I met the rest of the cast in a truly professional capacity for the first time this month. It was in a huge room at a local theatre in Notting Hill. Myself, Hugh Grant, Colin Firth, Liam Neeson and Emma Thompson were all there to do a read-through of the script and give ourselves and Richard an idea of how it would all work. Everyone had name places and, of course, I was sat next to the gorgeous Mr Grant. We were then given call sheets telling us when and where we would be needed in the next few months.

With rehearsals underway, we could get cracking with the filming, which was based mainly at Shepperton Studios with some location work around Dulwich and Wandsworth. I became good friends with everyone and tried really hard to take it all in and remember everything – I was working with people I'd admired for a long time. The thing that never ceases to amaze me is how generous and down-to-earth true stars are. It was once said to me that it's little people that have big egos, big stars don't need it because they have talent. And that was certainly true of this bunch. Silly things like reading the script in front of everyone can make you feel very nervous, and you can stumble over the simplest of sentences. They made it all

I just loved my 1970 Mercedes 280SL – shame it kept breaking down.

look so easy and I realised that, however much experience I've gained for someone of my age, I'm really just a beginner.

August was proving incredibly busy. Apart from rehearsals for *Love Actually*, I had to fit in lots of other things. I needed to get down to see Philip Treacy, who was designing my hat for the cover of my forthcoming album, *Musicality*. Philip's a delight and the hat was stunning – I loved it. It was a beautiful red and was sequinned all over. The sequins made it quite heavy, but it was so fabulous I didn't care.

I also made a trip over to Belfast to do the Patrick Kielty show. I had a fab time over there. I love going over to Ireland, the people are so warm and wonderful, and I actually made a second trip, this time to appear on the Daniel O'Donnell show. Mum came and we all had a great time once again. We went for dinner afterwards with Daniel and his lovely fiancée and chatted away for hours. Nanny was due to come with us, as she's a huge fan – in fact the main reason I agreed to do the show was so that she could meet Daniel – but she got a chest infection at the last minute and had to cancel. Daniel was lovely, he called Nanny and spoke to her on the phone. It made her night and certainly made her feel loads better.

Late in August, I had the opportunity to return to an old haunt of mine. As I've explained, I was born in London's East End, and my favourite market is on Roman Road. My mum used to have a dried flower stall down there and she knows most of the traders. I decided one Saturday to take a trip down memory lane with Alan – he was born and bred around there – and we took along my friend Sara Spa so we could go on a shopping spree. That isn't Sara's real surname, but she works in a spa so it's what I call her – genius, aren't I?!

It was a smashing day, and everyone welcomed me with open arms and sent their love to Mum. I bought some fabulous silver jewellery and a few gorgeous little tops. I wandered down the road feeling safe and secure back in the East End. Alan was great at keeping the crowds at bay, and I laughed non-stop with the stallholders. I was brought up in Hackney and went to school at Shacklewell Lane before getting a place at Italia Conti when I was ten years old. It made me very streetwise and I knew all about the 'real world' at a very young age. It's definitely a tough area – but I learned a lot and loved growing up round there. There are so many different types of people and what you see is what you get. I'll never forget my roots. But it was weird going back – as much as I know I don't truly belong in Kensington where I live now, I don't feel like I belong in the East End any more either, because the character of the East End I once knew is changing – and not for the better. Hopefully I'll create my own home when I decide to settle down and have a family some day, whenever that may be. In the meantime, I've moved around for most of my life, so I enjoy being a gypsy!

The first read-through for Love Actually with unknowns Hugh Grant and Liam Neeson

(oh my God!)

Clockwise from far left: With Richard Curtis. I'll never forget Richard for casting me in a movie most actresses would have killed for. Thanks, Rich!

Emma Freud, who stopped me getting to the set on time with all her naughtiness – you could often hear Richard asking where we were and what were we up to. I adore them both.

Whilst filming *Love Actually*, the streets were full of the local crowds, dying to get a glimpse of the stars of the film. We all had a good giggle while the cameras and lighting were being set, and I got to kiss my leading man off screen as well as on. The question people ask me most is did I enjoy kissing Hugh Grant? What do you think!

Opposite:
Me and my film family in *Love Actually*.

On the set of Downing Street in Love Actually

SECRET

Page 79/79

TREASURY DEPARTMENT

	1. ATTENTION IS DRAWN TO THE NOTES ON THE INSIDE FLAP	DIVISION
	2. ENTER NOTES OF RELATED FILES ON PAGE 2 OF THIS JACKET	13/79
		FOR REGISTRY USE ONLY

Registered file number

M/T79010eR

Date opened

8.11.02

SUBJECT

NHS SPENDING

Referred to	DATE	Department	CODE	Referred to	DATE	Referred to	DATE
	6.11	T10/001					
	8.11	T9/13					
	.11	T13/002					

It's a strange life. Things tick along for a while and then, all of a sudden, everything goes crazy. And this month was no exception – September looked busier than ever.

My album was still proving a worry, and my record company still wasn't showing quite the enthusiasm I expected. We were in September and I still didn't have an A&R man, which was really important, and I was concerned. A&R stands for Artist and Repertoire and these guys help you make decisions about the things that really matter – like the music. They help source the songs and find the producer and the studios. They manage the whole musical side.

After all I'd gone through, I knew I needed to record an album that would show I really could sing. A musical album had been a project I'd wanted to pursue for years. When I was at Italia Conti, our singing classes featured musical numbers as well as classical arias. Even before *My Fair Lady*, I wanted to record some songs like these, hoping to encourage a younger generation to listen to these classics. The public had already been introduced to me singing these songs when I sang 'Wouldn't It Be Lovely' and 'Don't Rain on My Parade' on the BBC's *Children In Need* show. It now seemed only natural to make an album of such timeless classics.

September

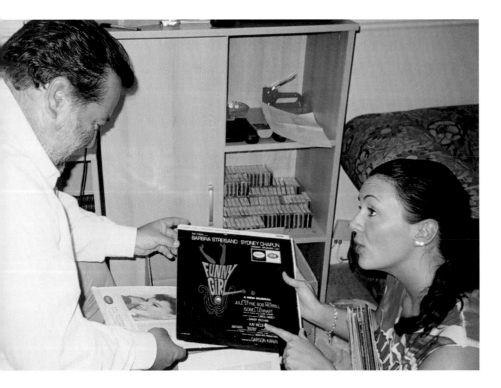

News finally reached me in the *Love Actually* rehearsals that they'd appointed an A&R man for my album. I'd met Mark Fox before and, to be honest, on first impressions I wasn't too sure, but as the meeting progressed I really grew to like him. For a start, he was excited about the project and that was a welcome change. He also had some great ideas regarding who I could work with, so we decided to give it a go.

Later I also met up with my album producer, Nigel Wright, and together we made a trip to diva heaven. We played lots of old vinyl records and they took me right back to my childhood, when I used to play those records and drift away into my own little world.

As usual, everything was going on at the same time. As well as rehearsals for the film and album I now needed to find time for the TV show, which was finally coming together – even if it wasn't what I'd expected. I'd agreed to do the show after a fabulous meeting at The Lanesborough hotel with the production company. I was very excited with some of the ideas for the show. The producer had worked with me before on a documentary that covered my life around the time my debut single, 'Perfect Moment', was launched. The show was a big success and got great ratings. Ideas included singing at prestigious venues such as Carnegie Hall and the Royal Albert Hall. I was relieved as they were just the sort of locations I wanted for the TV concert. We were on the same wavelength.

I've known music producer Nigel Wright for many years and it was a pleasure finally to be working with him. He has the most amazing record collection and on our first meeting we just listened to hundreds of old vinyl records, getting inspiration for the track list.

At the same time as meeting Nigel, I did a voice-over for my character Martoon, who appears on my website martinesplace.com.

I was really disappointed when I ended up with one of the BBC's studios in White City (so glam)! I've got no complaints about the set or the dancers – both were fabulous – but Carnegie Hall felt a million miles away …

The month turned into an endless round of appointments. While *Love Actually* took priority over everything else, the album needed lots of attention too. I had to attend the final dress fittings and make-up sessions for the film. I was having everything made specially for me and it took longer than I anticipated to get it all perfect. I also needed to find time to get recordings done for the album. This is a long process at the best of times, but we were using a live orchestra and needed to work alongside them, make sure the musical arrangements were right. We needed to book them all at the same place at the same time and also get my vocals down. At the same time I was still fulfilling the press and promotional commitments that had already started for the album. Jaine and William, my management team, were finding it hard to track me down – I couldn't answer their queries while I was filming or singing. The whole diary was too packed for any one person to fulfil and I felt really tired. I believe in having a personal life as well as working, but even I was finding it hard to juggle everything, and it was really starting to get me down.

With Nigel and Simon Lee at Sony Studios, trying out the new arrangements before I record with a 70-piece orchestra. Nigel was a magician who brought out the very best in me; we worked together as a team and loved the results. At every turn a new idea would develop, and we had a wonderful time turning various ideas into reality.

Clockwise from far left: The *Irish Post* Awards. Don't let the accent fool you, I've always been proud of being a Paddy!

Ronan won Best Recording Artist and I won Best Actress. We were both thrilled.

Mick McCarthy, who'd won an award. There was a lot of controversy between him and Roy Keane at the time, so there was a scrum of press around him. When he saw me he shouted: 'Martine, I didn't know you were a Paddy!' I asked if I could have a photo for this book provided I sent him a copy, which I haven't done yet. Sorry, Mick.

Dermot O'Leary has interviewed me many times over the years and we've always had a laugh, so it was nice to hang out with him socially. He was another award winner.

Months before, I'd had a call from my friend Dee. She'd been approached by the *Irish Post* who wanted me to attend their annual awards – and possibly even win one. Naturally – you guessed it – it was scheduled for this month. I really didn't want to miss it, though, so I went, taking Alan and Glyn along as security.

It was a lovely evening. The venue was the Park Lane Sheraton and as usual the press were waiting outside, cameras at the ready. I was nominated in the Best Actress category and I was delighted to win. There were loads of well-known faces there that night, Mick McCarthy and Ronan Keating to name but two. A wonderful evening was had by all, and I thoroughly enjoyed myself.

My highlight of the month, however, was my first day of filming *Love Actually*. I was very excited and couldn't sleep the night before. It was an early call, around 5am, and I was foggy-headed but I won't ever forget driving into Shepperton Studios for the first time – I felt like it was my first day at school. Would I come up with the goods? Would I even be noticed next to such a fabulous cast? Emma Thompson was really lovely to me – I can't rave about her enough. She made me feel right at home as a movie star.

We were filming a huge scene, set in an airport, and it included nearly all the cast. Everyone had cups of coffee and we all kept warm in big, padded location coats. Richard Curtis gave me a massive hug and asked if I was looking forward to my first day. 'Of course,' I replied. 'Take a look around, I'd be mad if I didn't!' I took a step back in order to soak in all that was going on. I wanted the day to stay with me for ever.

The only thing I don't like about filming is the early mornings. I would often be picked up around 5am to be in make-up and costume for 6am The days are long and there's lots of waiting around, but I normally take that chance to learn my

The first day of filming *Love Actually* with Emma Thompson, a double Oscar winner and the most gracious person I know.

Ben, one of the assistant directors, goes through the day's shooting schedule. We sometimes started at five o'clock in the morning and didn't finish until late in the evening, but I loved every second.

Love is the message on *Love Actually* in the make-up truck. We spent a morning deciding how my character's hair and make-up should be.

Love is the message on Love Actually.

scenes for the next day and catch up on boring things like bills and other everyday tasks. I'd be filming my part quite intensely for a few days and then have a couple of days off, then be filming again. Other than the first few days, when we were shooting that big scene with most of us in it, most of my scenes were with Hugh.

The whole process of finishing a film takes ages. When the actors have done their bit, there's still all the editing to do and the soundtrack. We're really just a tiny part of the process. One of my favourite days of filming was a scene where myself and Hugh are caught kissing by the press and an audience of hundreds (you'll have to watch the film to see why). We decided to film the audience's reaction for real – they didn't know what was going to happen and the response was brilliant. Kissing Hugh wasn't bad either! I kept joking with Richard, saying we didn't truly 'feel' that one and could we go again?

The wonderful Liam Neeson. Unfortunately I had no scenes with him, but at least we shared a make-up artist.

The man all the girls fall in love with ... Colin Firth.

The last day of filming
and I'm heartbroken it's over.
I wanted it never to end.

At Julien MacDonald's show – sitting in the front row with Ioan Gruffudd.

Taking time out from work that month, I headed off to Julien MacDonald's latest fashion show, which was in London this time. I adore Julien – over the years we've become very close. We talk for hours on the phone and he makes me feel wonderful. Julien has a wonderful ability to make any woman look amazing: sexy, glamorous and elegant all in one go. As far as I'm concerned (and many of the fashion press agree) Julien is up there in the top five best designers in England and you only need to go to one of his shows to realise that. All the top models love to be in his shows and everyone looks forward to them, season after season.

As usual, Julien put me in the front row, where I met up with Ioan Gruffudd again. I've met him at numerous castings and he's a delight, extremely handsome and very nice to be with socially. Also seated with us was the elegant Joely Richardson – a very beautiful lady. Naomi Campbell, who had gone through a really tough time of late, strutted her stuff magnificently at the show, and the whole evening was a real treat.

Another Magazine had its launch this month, and this time I headed for Clerkenwell with Linzi. It's a biannual magazine that uses high-quality and alternative photographers and journalists, and is owned by Rankin and Jefferson Hack. I've known Rankin for many years and he's photographed me on many occasions, including a shoot for *ES Magazine* while I was playing Tiffany. The evening came about purely by luck, as I had been filming all day and Linzi called me on the off chance. I dashed home to make it in time, got ready in fifteen minutes, and joined Linzi for the party. I stuck on an old Chinese top with jeans as it was one of those 'Too Cool for School' parties, and arrived at the entrance to be greeted by paparazzi both outside and inside.

The Elle Style Awards

September is the month for the *Elle* Style Awards, which were being held at the Natural History Museum, round the corner from my flat. I'd managed to get a stunning vintage dress for the event but I didn't think I was going to make it — I was filming late that day as we were running behind schedule. Luckily, however, we managed to contact the organizers who said they would give it another twenty minutes before they started the ceremony. There was also another artist running late and they wanted us both there.

It was a really fun evening, there were so many old friends there. It gave me the opportunity to play catch-up with some of my pals such as Blue, Gareth Gates, Nick Moran, Rhys Ifans, and Sam McKnight. It was a great night out. The winners included Kylie Minogue and Stella McCartney — two women I have lots of admiration for.

Standing between Nick Moran and Rhys Ifans at the *Elle* Style Awards. I'd been filming all day and didn't think I would make it through the night. I'd had a quick shower in the Winnebago and tried to get my dress on in the back of the car. I think I scrubbed up quite well, considering. Nick and Rhys wanted me to pass on dirty jokes to Hugh Grant — I forgot the punch lines, of course.

Clockwise from far left: Alex Sibley and I realized we had some mutual friends in Essex, as I tried to sober him up with glasses of water. He's so funny and a one-off. He is very realistic about *Big Brother* and what it can and can't do for you – he didn't let it go to his head.

Me and James Gooding.

With Duncan from Blue and Gareth Gates – he's cute, and taller than I thought.

Me and Rhys Ifans strike a pose – he gave me loads of great advice when I first went to LA.

Off duty at the Covent Garden Hotel.

Jonathan Barnham is my old boyfriend. I dated him for three years and was best friends with him for two years before that and, despite what people say, we don't hate each other. So it was good to see him on his birthday this month and catch up over a spot of afternoon tea at Claridges. We all need to move on in life, but it's nice to know that people can remain civil. Little did I know that this would fuel the press into believing I was chasing after him – the speculation really shocked me because such a thing would never happen. We had some nice times, but it's in the past and as a couple we're definitely over.

Meetings had been scheduled at the Covent Garden Hotel to discuss my website, along with various matters concerning my album. The day went swiftly, and Linzi and I decided to stay at the hotel, booking into the same suite that Glenn Close had stayed in the night before. We had loads of pink champagne and indulged ourselves with strawberries and hot chocolate sauce. Yummy! We'd sent out for some CDs and, with girly company, beauty products and fabulous music playing in the background, it was a special night.

The next day, I decided to pop down to Aldo Zilli's for a charity do. Aldo is a fabulous restaurateur and Italian chef. I met him years ago in the *EastEnders* days when he threw a birthday bash for me at one of his restaurants in Soho. Capital Radio were there – as was Chris Tarrant, one of my favourite people. I've met him at many charity events over the years and I also knew him through Capital when I was doing promotion for my albums. There were loads of paparazzi around that day, which helped give coverage to the good cause.

My Philip Treacy hat had arrived for the cover of my album. I instantly fell in love with it.

Soon after that, my Philip Treacy hat arrived and it was gorgeous. Unfortunately I got a spot on the day of the photoshoot – probably due to the indulgence of champagne and strawberries. It was being done at the Café de Paris, a venue I've always loved the look of and where I sang when I released 'Perfect Moment'. The cover turned out fabulously – me and my gorgeous red hat! The other photographs were so good we used them for the DVD cover too.

We still needed more rehearsals for the album and they took place at Sony Studios in Whitfield Street, in the West End. I listened to the all orchestral arrangements to make sure I was happy with everything. This kind of thing takes a lot of time – I'm a perfectionist, as are Nigel Wright and Simon Lee, my conductor. But our deadline was getting closer and we needed to get a move on. Listening to the arrangements was absolutely amazing. Up till now they'd been pre-recorded on tape and heard in the studio, but this time I had the pleasure of hearing the orchestra live. Sometimes I would go in the studio and sing for them so they could get the timing exactly how I wanted it when I put my final vocal track down. It was an amazing feeling – all those musicians just for me.

My stylist came over to my flat to decide what outfits we could create for the cover of the album. We wanted old-style glamour but we also wanted to keep it sexy and young. She brought with her a copy of *Vogue* and there I was!

Posing for the cover of *Musicality*. Little did you know I was standing on a box wearing a rolled-up top and old tracksuit bottoms!

The launch of Dale Winton's autobiography. Recording of the album was well under way and I was shattered, so I plastered on make-up to make myself look human.

My great friend Dale Winton had his book launch this month. I met Dale when we recorded a programme together about seven years ago. I love his sense of humour, his knowledge and loyalty. He's always there should I need a shoulder to cry on and he doesn't give a monkeys what anyone thinks. He's sometimes a nightmare, though, as he's always busy and we usually miss each other for lunch, but he's easily forgiven! The launch was very successful – as was the book itself. I was really proud of him.

This was the month I signed the deal for my new picture-led diary, which you're reading now. Having met several publishers I found HarperCollins were the ones for me and the rest, as they say, is history. I knew that writing the book was going to be incredibly hard work – documenting your life for a year is no easy task. I also wanted the final book to look different, incorporating lots of photos that would show my life over the year – and not just glossy pictures but plenty of snapshots too, capturing real moments as they happened. Mac had been photographing me for the past few months already, and the people at Kodak had generously agreed to supply the huge amount of film we would need for the year.

October

Singing star, actress and publishing sensation! The book deal is signed.

Discussing the design of this book with literary agent Robert Kirby at The Lanesborough hotel.

Sorting the photos for the book.
I'm not the most organised of people,
so it was a bloody nightmare.

October

Since the weather for October seemed to be holding out, I decided I could do with a weekend break. I invited Linzi, Mac and KG – another very good friend – for a weekend playing golf. We'd never played before but I decided it would be refreshing to do something totally different – or maybe I'm just getting old! We went to the golf club where *Goldfinger* was filmed, and each of us used the name of a character from the film to reserve our rooms. As we arrived, the receptionist asked, 'Miss J. Bond?', 'Mr Goldfinger?', 'Erm ... Jaws?' and finally 'Miss Pussy Galore?' 'That's me!' said Linzi. It was hysterical. KG and Mac are now totally hooked on the game of golf. Mac's obsessional, he loves it. Linzi and I just raced the golf buggies. A really fabulous weekend.

October was going to prove very busy with recording the album. I went along to Olympic Studios in Barnes and started to put down some final vocals. They were a fab team at the studios and very supportive – I felt marvellous and they really boosted my confidence. The songs were extremely familiar and each time I sang it felt better and better. I just wished at the time that I felt comfortable with my record company. The situation was beginning to cause real friction between me and my management company because nothing seemed to be running smoothly. By this time the record company had decided to give me a separate marketing team, something they said would be a good move, although I had my doubts. I was very frustrated and took a lot of my frustration out on my management team.

I'm quite a 'hands on' person, I believe in the saying that if you want something done right, then you need to do it yourself. This unfortunately means I spend a lot of my time on relatively minor matters that result in me getting very stressed. Although people do try to help me, it sometimes makes things worse. I've been accused of being difficult to work with, and perhaps to an extent that's true, but it's only because things have to be right for me – after all, if they aren't, it's me who takes the flak. I'm a professional, everything has to be perfect in my eyes to give the public what they pay for.

At the same time that I was recording the album, I also had to oversee my TV special. The show would be filmed for release as a DVD and video including additional backstage footage. All this was extra promotion for the album, it would all help. I'd ended up with a studio at the BBC, and we'd be lucky if we could afford all the musicians needed on the budget we'd been given, if we wanted to have a nice set and dancers too. Hardly the Royal Albert Hall or helicopters! It was very disappointing – my enthusiasm for the project was starting to dwindle.

When everything is going wrong, the best therapy is retail! I often meet up with my friend Sara Spa. We spend hours chatting and shopping and we have a great laugh together. We both decided we were fed up being single, and men were

My first ever film was *Kiss Kiss Bang Bang* with Chris Penn. I played a wonderful character called Mia, thanks to the casting by producer James Richardson and writer and director Stewart Sugg. James and I have remained great friends and have a spot of lunch now and again.

only a distraction, but a trip down the King's Road and Sloane Street worked wonders. We also popped over to Notting Hill and bought some lovely slippers from a small boutique. Now we never take them off, they're so comfy!

Vingt Quatre on Fulham Road.

It was 1 a.m. and I was tired
and pissed off as there were more
problems with the record.

I needed to sleep on it.

By the start of this month, everything was becoming very heavy what with the stress of filming, putting together the album and TV show, and all my other commitments. Communications were at breaking point and I needed help. Mum came up with the idea of getting a personal assistant on board and suggested my old friend Antony Read, who'd done the job with me before. Antony comes from Birmingham, though he's lived in London for many years. We've been friends for a long time, but in the past our friendship has suffered due to the pressures of working together. So this time we were determined not to let work get in the way, to keep work and friendship separate. Hurrah!

November

It's always difficult asking someone to come in halfway through a project. It puts other people's noses out of joint, and I think Jaine and William, my management, found it really difficult. To be fair to everyone, Jaine had never managed anyone in this capacity before. She was finding it hard and so was I. Jaine is a wonderful person, and a true family friend, but events had overtaken us. Life behind the scenes isn't easy, especially when there's so much going on. There were tears, arguments and conflicts, but we all had to pull together and get the job done – and ultimately, no matter what the problem, she battled for me all the way. Thanks, Jaine.

Jaine received a call asking if I would present the National Music Awards. It was a brand new show with Jeff Thacker as producer. I'd worked with Jeff in the past and we had got on very well. I first got to know him about five years ago when I worked on a show called *Abba Mania* that my friend Denise Van Outen was hosting and Jeff produced. He has great energy and knows exactly what he wants – he really stood out even then and was so accommodating.

As usual, I hated to turn down something I knew I might enjoy so I agreed to present the awards, despite my schedule. It was my first time presenting and I felt a bit nervous at the prospect. When we arrived for rehearsals, the autocue was too far away for me to see because I'm short-sighted, and for technical reasons they couldn't move it. Everyone nags me about having corrective surgery, but when do I get the chance?

This picture makes me howl with laughter

Jeff Thacker, a producer and good friend at Carlton TV, had asked me to present the National Music Awards and said I could close the show with one of my own musical numbers. I have great respect for him and he has given me wonderful advice over the years, so I accepted and thought it would be fun. It was my first ever presenting job and I was nervous. What didn't help was that I'm blind as a bat and had broken my glasses so couldn't see the autocue. We rushed to the opticians to get a pair of new ones and I wasn't happy: dresses and glasses just don't go.

Glasses seemed to be my only option. I had a fabulous gown to wear on the night and I tried to find a pair of glasses to match. Of course, if anything was going to go wrong, it was bound to involve me and, yes, the autocue broke down. With a packed audience, there was no choice for me but to ad lib. Jeff was obviously worried but I told him I would be OK. Every time I went off stage, we scribbled notes to help prompt me. It's the side the public never get to see, thank God! After all the acts had performed and collected their awards, the autocue was repaired and we all had to stay for another hour while I read it all again. Oh, the joys of entertainment!

To help promote the show, I did interviews non-stop for three days. Meanwhile I was still filming *Love Actually*. I still hadn't finished recording my album and there was one last song to sing, 'The Winner Takes it All'. Straight after a long day's filming for *Love Actually*, I made my way to producer Nigel Wright's studio in Surrey. All the way down there, agents, TV companies and management were on the phone, unhappy because I hadn't returned their calls. I was playing a bloody tea girl in Downing Street all day and I wasn't allowed to take my mobile phone on set, but no one seemed to understand that. I was being shouted at from every angle. Still in the car, I hung up the phone and broke down in floods of tears. Even

Leaving to go home. I kept my throat covered as there were lots more live gigs coming up.

More TV promotion for the album. I loved doing *Today with Des and Mel* (Dale was stepping in for Des while he was away). Out of all the promotional work it was the show that most people mentioned, so I'm glad I did it.

Next day it all got too much, as we were still trying to finish the album. Everyone wanted me everywhere and I was exhausted and frustrated. Glyn, my driver, snaps a glamorous point in my life.

Glyn, my driver, got emotional: 'Hang on a minute, Mart, give us your camera. Let's show everyone what it's really like.' I look at that picture and even now it makes me want to cry.

When I went into the studio that day Nigel could see I was upset. I put all my emotion into singing and recorded 'The Winner Takes it All' in three takes, in about fifteen minutes. Nigel laughed and said I should feel sad more often! At last the album was nearly finished and Nigel and I listened to it. I felt so proud. I knew it wasn't everyone's cup of tea, but I'd desperately wanted to do this album and I had to show everyone my voice was back. It felt like a major personal and professional accomplishment. After we'd sorted out the running order and listened to the whole thing in a studio in Chelsea a couple of weeks later, the album was finally completed. And if I do say so myself – it was bloody brilliant!

When you're feeling stressed and everything seems to be going wrong, the best

thing to do is to meet up with a mate. Sara Spa rang and we decided to go for dinner. I have a favourite Chinese restaurant in the King's Road, and we headed there for a girly night. We tried so hard to have fun but the phone kept ringing non-stop throughout the meal. I was tempted to switch it off but I couldn't because I knew important things were going on and there would be decisions to make.

I got a call from the lovely Conor, who works with my agent Paul Lyon Maris at ICM, the agency that represents me for acting work. I'd been invited to read for another film part. I loved the character, and it seemed like a brilliant film. Everything went really well and I met up with producers and directors. Unfortunately, the other leading lady pulled out and the project was shelved for the moment. What a shame, but that's show business.

Until you're established as a movie star, it's very rare just to get offered a role with no screen test. I can't bear them. When I've got the job I'm happy – with the

My bosoms have often been discussed in the press, and a friend of mine thought this T-shirt was pretty appropriate. I was having a fabulous dinner with my friend Sara, and then, uh-oh, another call.

The Frank Skinner show was great fun and good promotion for the forthcoming album. Me, Frank and Harry Hill decided to sing 'Wouldn't It Be Lovely' at the end of the show. I knew Frank's sharp wit could make guests nervous and I was no exception, but Frank was very kind to me and he loves musicals. Hurrah!

sets, the other actors and the costumes it's difficult not to feel the part – but when you're in a tiny room with just a camera and a casting director it can feel really weird, especially if you're saying your lines with a woman and she's supposed to be Keanu Reeves or someone like that! I've been for so many auditions in my life and yet, no matter how long I've been at it, they always make me nervous. I often come out of them forgetting everything – what I said, what I did, what I looked like. For any budding actress or singer out there, the best thing you can do after a casting is to simply forget it. Nine times out of ten you're trying to fulfil an exact picture of what the director or writer or producer has in their head and the chances are you'll rarely be perfect. But keep going, build up your confidence and experience, and who knows? One day you could land that dream job. That's the thing I love about this industry – one phone call can change your life for ever.

I was booked to do the Frank Skinner show this month but I was nervous at the thought. Frank had appeared on *Never Mind the Buzzcocks* but, if I recall, wasn't too complimentary about me! Despite that, he was fair when he interviewed me, and we ended up having great fun. Harry Hill was another guest on the show and he was extremely funny that night. Finally we all dressed up and sang 'Wouldn't It Be Lovely' from *My Fair Lady*, just for a laugh. Who would have thought that one day I would feel so much better about the whole *My Fair Lady* experience that I could even sing one of the songs for fun? At last it was easy again.

November was going to be a really big month. The album was about to be released and the musical show would be on TV. It was stressful to say the least. The show was a very important part of the promotion for the album, and I wasn't happy with the way it was going. To make matters worse, there was a flu bug going round and, just as I was to start rehearsals, I caught what started out as a mild cold. Jaine, my manager, had it and so did Antony, my PA, so we were really in the wars! I was absolutely fine to continue with the show but the TV company started panicking. I can't help but believe that sometimes people had read too much rubbish about *My Fair Lady* in the past and this was, perhaps, letting it affect the decision about the TV show. I thought they were going to pull the show after I asked for one day off from rehearsals. I pick up routines quickly and I'd spoken with the choreographer, who said it was fine. After all, the dancing was pretty basic for me as I was singing big numbers. The choreographer had also mentioned that a couple of the dancers had flu and didn't want me to catch it. I simply had a head cold and knew that to keep warm and look after myself for a day would make all the difference. If I didn't know what would make me better then no one did. But, still, I had to attend. Either I turned up, or there would be no show. I knew this but it didn't make me feel any better.

Andrea Bocelli was going to duet with me on my TV special, but he wanted me to sing in French. It has been a long time since I had sung classically and I had a cold. I felt everyone was blowing the whole thing out of proportion, as they were convinced I was at death's door. I promptly panicked too, although I knew that I was completely capable of performing. So I sat on the stairs and practised while waiting for Bocelli's people to arrive, then I sang it through with a marvellous voice coach who got the very best out of me. As a result Bocelli was pleased with what he heard and accepted my invitation on to the show. Singing with him was the most magical time of my career, I'll never forget it. The TV company was happy too – phew!

Picture the scene. There I was at rehearsals. My doctor had been to visit me and ordered me to bed, but the schedule wouldn't allow for it, so there I was, high-kicking my legs and being taught all the dance moves for the numbers that needed a bit of choreography to give them that old musical feel. I arrived with Antony, coughing and sneezing and saying 'This is bloody madness!' Then I had to get to a meeting with Andrea Bocelli's people to learn the duet I was to sing with him in French. Of course, after dancing for hours my voice was starting to go.

Bocelli is an amazing talent and naturally he'll only perform alongside someone who has what he considers to be a proper voice. I went into the studios to record. I waited for an agonising length of time. My voice was there. Alleluia! His people seemed very happy so we decided to arrange the song there and then. We would put down the bits I could sing and leave the parts he would be singing, then we could listen to it and both know what we were doing on the day.

I've had many wonderful moments in this business, but recording and singing with Andrea Bocelli has to be the highlight. He's very calm and he has the voice of an angel. He moved me so much, I wanted to stay next to him and enjoy every moment. That duet will stay with me for ever.

Finally it was time to record the TV show in front of a live audience. Although I was feeling tentative because there had been so many problems, it was time to

Recording and singing with Andrea Bocelli was the highlight.

show everyone what I could do. By now the album had been delivered to EMI and I knew this was going to be a very important period for me.

Along with the public who went to the TV show recording, my mum had invited a special audience consisting of numerous family and friends. The organisers from the TV company were obviously having problems that night – instead of reserving seats for my friends and family, they had filled them with members of the public. This wouldn't have been a problem, except that I needed to know where my special guests were because we were filming and they were included in the script. But we finally got it sorted and all the guests were happy.

The usual suspects were all there that night: Mum and Alan, Auntie Kim and all my friends and family, including the Tanners. Goalkeeper David Seaman was also there with his wife Debbie, as was Graeme Le Saux and his wife. My doctor was in the audience, he had been so supportive over the last year and I thought he deserved a night off. I'd also invited my old school teacher, Ann Smith, and arranged a special treat for her by speaking about her and dedicating one of my songs to her. Unfortunately, this bit didn't appear in the final televised version, but it was included in the DVD and video that were brought out afterwards.

The night began with a warm-up man on stage, to get the audience into a good mood while I prepared for my performance. Jan, my dresser, added the finishing touches to my outfit and, after a gulp of hot water and lemon, I was on. The applause was tremendous and I felt on top form. I opened the show with 'Diamonds Are a Girl's Best Friend' and as I finished the number, I felt things were going to be all right. The audience was marvellous. A competition had been held via the website for a fan to attend the show, and Chris Johnson from Coventry had won. I was delighted for him – he's been a massive fan of mine for a long time and he'd wanted to meet me for ages. I had a chat with him during breaks in recording and he eventually got his wish to meet me properly later, at the after-show party. Chris, it was a pleasure!

The set for the show was truly marvellous. Its main features were a series of elegant hanging lights and a sweeping staircase that gave it a real Forties, Fred Astaire and Ginger Rogers feel. There was a full live orchestra conducted by the wonderful Simon Lee. It's worth stressing here that the show was recorded live, so it was more like a live concert, with nothing covered up or hidden. I sang and danced every dance live – the only advance recording was with Andrea Bocelli, purely because of his schedule. The dancers were amazing, all perfectly rehearsed and looking stunning in their outfits of fishnets and corsets – so glamorous. They'd all mentioned how nice it felt to be dancing something so classic and theatrical for a change. Many of them had been doing pop work and touring with boy bands.

Vinnie Jones, who I've known for ages, had agreed to perform with me, and Graham Le Saux and David Seaman thoroughly enjoyed that part of the show. Vinnie was delighted to see them there and they shared a few jokes later. Vinnie is a real talent and he proved it that night when we sang 'Bad Boy Leroy Brown' to huge applause. My link with Judy Garland was another memorable part of the night. We used some old footage of a concert she'd sung and filmed in London, editing it so I could duet with her. We sang 'The Man That Got Away', a song she made famous in that all-time classic movie, A Star is Born. What an amazing lady she was. I must thank the Judy Garland Estate for giving its permission.

In another interesting segment of the show, they showed some old film of me performing as a nine-year-old. It was so funny to see myself up there, showing off and singing 'The Lady Is a Tramp'. Mum had found the video and we laughed and laughed as we watched it again – it brought back amazing memories. I told you I'd been singing these songs for years!

The show took just a few hours to record and everyone was happy with the results. The dancers had done a great job, as had all the background staff. I was really pleased with it – I knew I'd done everything I could to make it a success.

Rehearsals for the TV special were very intense. Not many people sing with such a large orchestra these days and I was humbled at how the set designer had managed to make the most of them. There were lots of sound checks, rehearsals, and the odd bit of pre-recording. I loved the choreography and the dancers were totally professional, they all took time out to teach me extra bits of the routines. The dress rehearsal was a nightmare at first. We had to make out we could do the changes quickly so the audience wouldn't get restless, but my look had to be exactly the same as in the pre-recordings. Continuity is always a killer. Andrea Bocelli had to fly out to Italy as soon as we had pre-recorded so I didn't get as much time with him as I would have liked.

I look back on that show with pride.

The TV studios had arranged an after-show drinks and nibbles party, so once everyone was assembled, I left the peace of my dressing room to join my guests. I was thrilled that so many people had waited to see me and give me their congratulations. After the party, I decided to finish the evening at the Wellington Club, where my close family and friends came to celebrate. Jake and Christian gave me a warm welcome and we all had a lovely night.

Very big thank yous have to go to Julien MacDonald, who made all my costumes for the show, and Maria Grachevogal for the red dress I wore for the opening number – it looked stunning while I sang 'Diamonds Are a Girl's Best Friend'. My last dress was a beautiful pink number with black ribbon. I felt a million dollars in it and just would not take it off. It became my party dress and everyone loved it – well, everyone but a certain tabloid that said I looked like a box of chocolates in it. Oh well, each to their own . . . I didn't care. I felt marvellous.

It's a funny thing, actually, but a sister Sunday paper to that particular tabloid had nothing but criticism for my show. Apparently my performance was dreadful, the stage sets were awful, in fact everything about the show was crap. They also claimed I sang off key all night, even with Bocelli. When I read that, I felt they were out to ruin everything. My mum put it into perspective, though, when she said 'It's only one man's opinion. If they knew what went into performing, maybe they would be kinder.' Nevertheless, even I was unprepared for such a negative review. I've watched the DVD since and I'm still very proud of my performance. The viewers proved they loved it too by buying it and making it a best-seller.

I look back at that show with pride. Despite a few run-ins I had with management, the TV company and the record company, I was proud of what I'd accomplished. After all, I'd been told it had the biggest viewing figures for that night and, despite some of the press, the public were writing and telling me how much they loved it. I now had to concentrate on promoting the album. It was going to mean more hard work, but Christmas was in sight and I was determined to be optimistic.

My album was due for release on 2 December. On the previous Saturday, Jaine rang to say she was concerned because we hadn't received any albums for promotion or even for our personal use. I found this unbelievable and asked her to call the record distribution office to get some albums for me, Antony and the management office. After days of arguing, the albums arrived a week later. Even more incredible, when Jaine received hers she found a box full of plastic CD covers with nothing in them. What was going on? Friends also did their usual rounds of the shops to see if the album was in stock, but where was it? I was told that even when they did find copies they were on the bottom shelves where they could hardly be seen. Nor had any signings been arranged. I felt I was fighting a losing battle.

When I looked around town, I could find no posters or promotion in the shops and there was hardly any airplay on the right radio stations. All right, it was a hard album to sell. Yes, there were big posters on buses and Virgin did pay for a TV advert. So, following the reports I was getting back from friends, I took it upon myself to look in some record stores to see if I was happy with the displays and the amount of albums they had in stock. I decided to go to Harrods as it's my local store (very posh!) but I was really embarrassed to find that I had no display whatsoever. I wasn't even included on the new releases shelves. Worse still, when I asked a shop assistant why this was the case, he did a computer check and explained that only five copies were in stock – not enough to do a display. The poor guy seemed embarrassed for me and, to be honest, I don't think I'd felt so humiliated for a long time. If you have a flop you've got to take it on the chin – but I just didn't feel that the album had been given the best possible chance. I was told later that there were no posters in the shops because of the time EMI/Liberty were given to arrange things.

I had a wonderful time with my record company and I'll always be thankful to Cheryl Robson, who was the A&R for 'Perfect Moment', and Hugh Goldsmith, who took a chance with a soap star and turned her into a number-one selling pop star. But everyone has to move on sometime and a lot of my team weren't at Virgin any more. Virgin weren't happy and I wasn't either. It was a natural decision to go our separate ways. I was a little bit sad, but to be honest, part of me was relieved. In any case, I now had the bug for movies!

After the show, with Debbie and David Seaman and Vinnie Jones. At last I was allowed my favourites: chocolate and champagne! When I sing I avoid both like the plague as they play havoc with my voice. Everyone knew how tough the whole process had been and we couldn't wait to celebrate, first in the BBC studios and then later in the Wellington.

My album still weighed heavily on my mind and I wanted to do whatever was necessary to try and improve sales. I couldn't just give up on it, could I? So I took it upon myself to do a signing at Harrods, and it was promptly booked for 12 December. I was determined to meet the fans and say a personal hello to everyone who turned up. I was really nervous as I had never arranged my own signing before and, after such poor sales, I didn't know if anyone would turn up!

But my fears were soon swept away as I walked into the music department. There were TV and film crews everywhere, along with a barrage of paparazzi and loads of loyal fans queuing with my CD in their hands. It was a two-hour signing, which included promotion of the album, the DVD and video of the show, as well as my new website. Moira Bellas, my publicist, was there to support me, along with Mum, Antony and Alan. The two hours passed very quickly and there was always a queue. I imagined what could have been if we'd done more events like this.

December

I had one more singing commitment as Jaine had arranged for me to sing at an annual ball. I'd been invited to sing at the Hodders Ball and agreed to do it. It turned out to be a fabulous evening, and I must thank them for inviting me to Barbados. What a fabulous time!

There was no point on dwelling on what could have been with the album. It was time to move on. Linzi and I had organised a 'black dress and black tie' Christmas party at The Belvedere restaurant in Holland Park, so all our friends could come along and enjoy themselves. The invites went out quite late but we were delighted that so many people accepted. The brilliant Marco Pierre White had given us the venue and champagne for the night, for which I'm very grateful. Antony, my PA, had employed five transvestite waitresses to serve people with drinks, and everyone agreed it was a fab idea – they entertained us non-stop. Thank you, girls!

The venue rapidly filled up. We'd nearly run out of cloakroom space while people were still arriving. The Belvedere was the perfect venue and everybody looked beautiful. Although there was a mix of family and friends there, as well as Linzi's fashion crowd and some well-known faces, everybody got on. The lovely Dale Winton arrived, as did Alex Sibley, Nicky Clarke and his beautiful wife, and many more. I was so pleased. It was one of the best parties ever. We had a piper who stood on the steps and piped the guests in. At the end of the evening I asked him to play a tune for my Scottish hairdresser, Mark Anderson, whose wee granny had recently passed away. He said it was a real tribute to her. The evening was such a success that we're thinking of making it a permanent fixture in the diary.

Now the year was nearing its end and I had Christmas to celebrate. I'd been seeing someone on and off for a few months, but I'd had to keep the relationship under wraps. James Gooding had been a good friend of Linzi's for years and he'd only recently finished a relationship, so he was still upset. (I don't need to mention who his girlfriend was as she has had enough press intrusion.) I'd met James on numerous occasions, we always had fun and he seemed to find me easy to talk to. And, yes, there had been an attraction there. But as December moved on, I became aware that he wasn't the man for me. He hadn't been completely honest about the end of his previous relationship and, despite press speculation, I would never want to share a man with anyone, nor do I think it's respectful. The minute I realised that might be the case, I knew it could only cause unhappiness for everyone and I ended it straight away. We shared some time together, but James's heart had obviously been broken – he seemed lost, like a time-bomb ready to explode at any moment. Needless to say, that's what eventually happened. It was a shame for everyone involved and, in the end, I think he let himself down.

I didn't want to dwell on that time – once I know someone isn't for me, I switch off.

Performing at the Hodders Ball. As usual I had to rush to get ready, so I stuck my hair back in a bun. Add a pair of Gina heels and a red dress and I was ready to go. Me and Jodie Kidd had a catch-up and a giggle.

The Parkinson Christmas special. I adore Michael, having first met him when I went on the show a year ago. His words of support, in public and in private, at the time of *My Fair Lady* were a huge comfort. He saw me in the show twice and loved it. He said it was one of the best shows he had ever seen and in his words I was 'magic'.

I hadn't had a serious relationship for a long time anyway, and to be honest, I hadn't felt ready. Men had asked me out on dates and the idea always seemed appealing, but the reality was that I wouldn't have known a good thing if it had stood up and bitten me on the nose. I needed time to be on my own and I learned a lot about myself in that time.

James Tanner had always been wonderful to me and I would be a liar if I said I didn't find him attractive from the moment I met him. He'd always been honest about what he felt and had been one of the best friends I'd ever had. I would often wish during the many times I spent with him that I felt ready for a relationship, but that would only happen with time. His romantic life had moved on just as mine had, but we still stayed in touch and around now we both found ourselves free from entanglements and able to meet up. Little did I know that later this month, during a shopping trip to Harrods with James, I'd find love welling up in me – I realised in that moment that maybe I was falling in love with him. It's amazing how you can look back on situations and recognise that love was staring you in the face all the time. We had a wonderful day together and I felt that James might have stronger feelings for me too – but for now, I decided to keep my emotions to myself.

Anyone who knows me will be aware how much I love Christmas. As a little girl I would get very excited at the prospect of seeing Santa Claus, putting up the tree and wrapping presents. And things haven't changed. Even at my age, I still expect Mum to fill my stocking. This year we decided to spend Christmas Day at my home and I was really pleased. Here was my chance to make everything look beautiful and welcome Mum and Alan, Auntie Kim, Mac, Linzi and Dale Winton.

Linzi had never experienced a proper Christmas before. She comes from Leeds and her family is Jewish. Linzi respects her religion, but she couldn't resist the opportunity to see what happens in a Christian household. She and Auntie Kim stayed on Christmas Eve, while the others were due to join us in the morning.

As usual we followed tradition. After wrapping a few last presents, we headed off to the church across the road for midnight mass where we all sang carols. I was singing my heart out as I always do, so much so that my attention was distracted. Suddenly Auntie Kim said in a loud whisper, 'Martine, your carol sheet is on fire!' I'd let my hand waver towards the candles – you can guess the rest ...

We made a quick exit and ran back to the flat. To end the evening, we had a champagne toast, hung up our stockings and went to bed. Just before falling asleep I received a lovely text from James wishing me a very merry Christmas.

The next day Mum and Alan left home extra early to ensure that they reached us before we woke up. The car was laden with presents, shopping, pots and pans –

Alistair McGowan and Chris Eubank celebrating Christmas after the Parkinson show. By the way, I was supposed to have blonde highlights, but ended up auburn.

and stockings, of course. Mum had decided to make Linzi a stocking too. They arrived at 7.45am and Kim was awake to greet them. As I lay in bed, I could hear them giggling in the corridor. Kim was already making bacon sandwiches, tea and coffee. Soon I couldn't stand it any longer. I woke Linzi up and in stockinged feet we cheered, sliding down my marble corridor like a pair of six-year-olds.

I'd recently had a wooden floor laid in my sitting room, and was really pleased with the look. It was also much easier for Sam, my cleaner, as I'm hopelessly clumsy and always spill drinks everywhere. Linzi and I sat in the middle of the floor, begging Mum to give us our stockings. Mum's very traditional, she always puts in nuts and fruit and a piece of silver, and the silliest presents ever. Linzi and I both received flashing Christmas earrings, sweet necklaces, snap playing cards, whoopee cushions and a variety of daft toys. I loved my stocking and Linzi was ecstatic with hers – it was a totally new experience for her.

Auntie Kim and Mum had been assigned dinner duties, while Alan was busy clearing the rubbish we'd already made. After breakfast, and once the turkey was in the oven, we all sat down together to open our presents. When I looked at the decorations on my Christmas tree I just had to giggle to myself. My friend Irene had agreed to help decorate it and had insisted on drinking champagne the whole time. She was totally blotto by the time she finished, but the tree looked fantastic. Irene is a brilliant woman I met eight years ago. She's the same age as my Mum and I've watched her children Hayley and Dan grow up. They feel like family to us and, along with their dad Chris, we think the world of them.

We all sat round together, drinking orange juice and eating chocolates, and I took charge of giving out the presents. Everyone began to rip off the wrapping paper and screams of delight echoed all over the flat. Mum was thrilled to get a new coat, Jimmy Choo shoes and an amazing assortment of bags, luxury toiletries and jewellery. Kim had new jumpers, shirts and hair appliances and Linzi and I had bought each other virtually identical presents. Alan loved his new shirts and jumpers and I adored all my 'smellies', especially the candles and room fragrances.

I put my candles in the fireplace to light them, and the room was soon filled with the smell of cinnamon and red berries. I could hear the church bells ringing and Mum and Kim busy in the kitchen, arguing as usual over the vegetables. Alan carried on clearing up, while Linzi was busy testing her presents. I took a deep breath and closed my eyes for a few seconds. God, I love Christmas. All that was really missing was LJ, who was spending Christmas with his dad, and James Tanner, who I missed very much.

Linzi and I showered and dressed before proceeding to lay the table. Now, I'm very fussy about my table. I had recently purchased a new table and chairs and I wanted it all to look beautiful. I had a large centrepiece entwined with ivy and

A snap of the paparazzi snapping me at Prada, Sloane Street, Christmas shopping.

Me and Dean Gaffney have our hair done at Daniel Galvin. I love him to bits – you deserve the best, Dean!

everyone had a pretty place setting. Mac arrived dead on time, looking very smart in his purple suit. We put on some new CDs, chatting and laughing. Meanwhile, Kim had taken control in the kitchen and chucked Mum out. Then my phone went and it was Dale. He couldn't make dinner as an emergency had come up. We would miss him, but dinner still went full steam ahead.

I was so pleased with the way everything looked. Dinner was nearly ready by now, and everyone was looking forward to a massive blow-out. I was really happy because James had called to wish me a merry Christmas. We were invited over to the Tanners' house that evening for a karaoke night, so I would get to see James and all his family. LJ had also phoned from his Dad's house. He was having a wonderful time, so now I was totally content.

As usual, something had to go wrong. Auntie Kim had forgotten to steam the vegetables and also forgot about the Yorkshire puddings in the oven, which left us all roaring with laughter. I'd put my hair in rollers to make sure it looked nice for the evening, and I posed for photos by the tree – I forgot about the roller in my fringe, though!

Christmas night at the Tanners'.

Mum and Linzi give me a run for my money.

Mac falls asleep after Christmas dinner at my flat (interesting choice of shoes!).

After dinner we all needed a little nap. Everyone was exhausted except Mum and Kim, who cleared up and carried on chatting. But by late afternoon it was time to get ready for our evening out. Mum looked a treat in her new coat. Linzi and I travelled in Mac's car and Kim went with Mum and Alan. As usual, as soon as we arrived south of the river we got lost, so James came down to meet us and guide us back to his parents' home.

There was a whole crowd at Pat and Terry Tanners', but we received a wonderful welcome and everyone was soon in party mood. The karaoke machine was busy that night. When it was my turn, Mum, Kim, Pat and Linzi decided to be my backing singers while I sang several numbers from *Musicality*. My singers soon turned into dancers and the whole house filled with laughter. We had a wonderful evening, and no one went to bed until five in the morning.

The next day we were due at the Tanners' again for Boxing Day dinner and we all managed to arrive on time. Dinner was wonderful. Mum especially enjoyed it as she finally got to eat some vegetables, which she loves. Boxing Day is a games day, so we decided to play the 'Post-It' game again. I couldn't believe it when James guessed who he was on the second question. 'Postman Pat!' he shouted with a massive grin on his face. We all looked at each other very suspiciously.

With the girls at Momo's, West London, enjoying the food in the restaurant upstairs and then taking over the club downstairs. We didn't stop cackling all night and we were nicknamed The Witches of Eastwick by the boys.

Suddenly it dawned on us – he'd cheated by looking into a mirror coffee table so he could see who he was. He was banned from playing, but I think he did it on purpose. He just wanted an excuse to join the rest of the guys in the kitchen.

All too soon Christmas was over and we all had to get back to normal. I spent those few days in between Christmas and the New Year with James. It had been obvious to everyone there was a real chemistry and we were very much in love. In those few days I had found the nerve to tell him how I felt. James had been so patient, he'd watched me get through all the obstacles I'd faced and waited for me with open arms. He had loved me unconditionally for a long time – something that hadn't happened to me with any man before. He was one of the strong ones and I didn't ever want to let him go. But I wasn't going to be with him for the New Year because his family always go away for the festivities. I could have gone too, but I'd arranged for us to join my friend Irene in the New Forest to celebrate. At least Mum and Alan, LJ and Linzi would be joining us. I knew LJ would love it, they have an indoor pool and there would be other children there.

Mum, Alan, LJ and Linzi all arrived at my flat and we got in the car to meet up with Irene in Chelsea. The plan had been to follow her down, but the weather was going to make it very difficult. There was torrential rain most of the way and our driver could hardly see where he was going, so we decided to take it slowly. Although the journey took longer than usual, at least we all made it in one piece.

Irene and Chris have a wonderful country home, and there were about thirty of us gathered there for the New Year celebrations. Irene had booked us into a local hotel, and before long we were changed and ready to party. Chris had cooked a traditional roast, there was wonderful music and a real feeling of welcome. In minutes LJ was in the pool, Mum was reading Irene's tarot cards and Alan was chatting with the men. I settled myself with Irene's lovely daughter Hayley. She's like a little sister to me and we're incredibly close. We chatted until the last few seconds of the year. Big Ben chimed and everyone joined hands for 'Auld Lang Syne'. Then the music really started and everyone was laughing and dancing. Tiredness hits people at different times, but eventually our little group were all exhausted. We made our way back to our hotel at around 2am and fell into bed. So wild, aren't I?!

The next day brought sunshine and showers. We went back to the house for coffee and then had a nice long walk in the country before going to the local pub for lunch. We wanted to head back to London before it got too dark, and Mum and Alan had an extra couple of hours' travel before they reached home, so we all said our goodbyes. But I knew I would see Irene in the next week or two. She was jetting off to Barbados and so was I.

Me and James Tanner.

Me

Linzi

Sarah

Hayley

It snowed on the Kings Road.

As usual I felt a little down after all the festivities. January is a long, cold month and I know everyone is happy when it's over. However, this was the month when I had to focus on getting this book you're reading sorted out, and I also had a day's filming to complete for *Love Actually*. I'd decided to set off for Barbados as soon as my filming commitments were fulfilled.

It was lovely to see everyone again for that last day on *Love Actually*. We hadn't managed to fit in all our scenes before Christmas and we had one exterior shot left to do. Hugh had been busy till now, too, so we got cracking and before I knew it, it was, as they say, a wrap. There had been a wrap party in December, but not many of the cast could make it due to other commitments. The last night of filming was special. There were more people than ever filling the streets, and there was a real buzz of excitement. The scene was lovely too – it went very well. Without giving the game away, the film finale is wonderful and it was a privilege to know and work with the entire cast and crew.

January

Barbados

It's January and time to play and rest the mind. Best friend Linzi comes along and forgets all about the fashion industry for two weeks. Unluckily for her, one newspaper mistook her for me and another claimed she was my double!

Once filming was over, I could concentrate on getting away. Linzi had never visited Barbados, so I couldn't wait to take her out there and show her all the fab places I now know so well. Barbados is a particularly special place for me because Mum and Alan got married there in January 2000. I wanted to treat them by arranging for them both to go back. Mum had managed to make a second visit since the wedding but Alan has always been too busy with work. This year, I'd hatched a plan to get them both out there and, thanks to Jaine, William and a lovely man called Stephen Grant, it worked. Stephen is a very good friend of the O'Haras who own the Coral Reef Club. I always stay there when I visit the island and Stephen had a villa close by, which he let Mum and Alan use. There are lovely people in this world after all!

Now, because everything I did this year was relevant to this book, I decided to get Mac out there too. He shared the villa with Mum and Alan and we all had a fantastic time. Mac had never visited Barbados either, so we had great fun showing him the sights. One of my favourite places is the Cliff restaurant, where I'd planned for us to eat on our last night. Meanwhile we enjoyed a fabulous dinner at Coral Reef and another great meal cooked for us by Maria at the villa.

The weather was glorious, so Linzi and I swam to the pontoon nearby and sunbathed all day. Mum and Alan, who both swim like fishes, ventured into the sea too. Mac, however, was like a brick when he got in the water, and just sank – he

top left:
Discussing the book with Mum.

top right:
With Sonique, at the Coral Reef Club, chilling out and having fun. She needed a break too.

I'm a great believer in doing what you want on holiday.

tried ever so hard, but to no avail! He did manage to capture some lovely shots on the beach though, at the Coral Reef Club and at the villa.

I'm a great believer in doing whatever you want on holiday, and I respect other people's personal time. Alan and Mum would wander down the beach, Mac would practise his golf, and Linzi and I would hire jet skis or go on a motorboat ride. We boarded a jet boat one day when the sun was blazing, both of us thinking it would be an ideal time to top up our tans. By the time we were out at sea, however, the clouds had come over, then the heavens opened up and we were bombarded with hailstones. It could only happen to us!

If there was a down side to my break in Barbados, it was the press intrusion into my private life. They followed me, hiding in trees and behind rocks to take their photos. The press accused Linzi of being my clone, but what was really funny was that the paparazzi out there actually mistook her for me several times. They even printed her picture in the paper saying it was me. Ha ha, got it wrong!

The press often love to get in remarks about whether I'm too fat or too thin. You can't please everyone, but I felt slim, healthy and happy out there, and I really don't care what they think any more. It's amazing how different you can look depending on what story they decide to go with. As you can see from our own camera shots, I look just fine.

Our last evening came around all too quickly. I'd already seen my friend Irene out there. She was having a fabulous time, but she was too tired for dinner on our last night. The Cliff restaurant was booked and so the five of us set off. The Cliff is built on three levels in the open air, almost like a tier cake, and I'd made sure we had a table in a good location for the evening. The waves wash up on the beach

At the Coral Reef Club after dinner, I tried my hand with the steel band. I hadn't had a pina colada, I promise.

I was up early to dash down to the beach and catch a last few hours in the sun.

I really didn't want to
go home.

below and there are twinkling lights everywhere. It's an amazing place and the
food and service are second to none.

We decided to go the whole hog that night: starters, main course and dessert,
with wine and champagne. We toasted Mum and Alan and, as we did so, my
thoughts turned again to James. Reading my mind, Mac said how much he was
missing his girlfriend and how lovely it would be to all visit there again, this time
with our partners. We made a little pact around the table to try and come back.
The evening was wonderful, the food was amazing and we all laughed and
chatted over coffee. It was perfect.

We finally headed back and I arranged to meet up with the others later the next
day. Linzi and I were booked on an earlier flight and the thought came into my
mind to stay a bit longer, but I knew I wouldn't be able to, due to work
commitments. I was up early the next day to dash down to the beach and catch a
last few hours in the sun. Linzi and I looked around: the place was paradise and
we were both going to miss it so much. I was sad, but also eager to get back and
see James. We'd called each other regularly in Barbados and soon I would be
seeing him in the flesh. Hooray!

January had passed quite quickly. When I arrived home on the 31st, it was very
cold and my poor James was on crutches. He'd injured himself playing football and
had been at the hospital for hours. We saw January out watching a video at home
and playing catch-up. I told him all about my holiday and he filled me in on his
news. It was wonderful to be back with him.

This month started off with a real celebration. Lino is a hairdresser at Daniel Galvin's in George Street. He always looks after me when I go there and over the years we've become very good friends. It was his wedding day today and he was marrying a beautiful lady called Artemis in a Greek wedding ceremony. I was thrilled for him and wouldn't have missed it for the world.

Mum and Alan joined me for the wedding, along with LJ. We arrived at the church just in time, making our way round to some empty pews. Steve McFadden and his girlfriend Lucy were there, and Lucy was as sweet as ever. Dean Gaffney – who I've always remained friends with – was there too with his lovely wife Sarah.

We all left the church after the ceremony to attend the reception at the Hilton. It was superb and there were loads of guests. Lino does many famous people's hair and most of them had turned out to see him married. I chatted with lots of people I hadn't seen in ages. Mum and Alan also said their hellos, but it was obvious that LJ was getting tired. By 10pm Mum, Alan and LJ had left, but I decided to stay on. William and Jaine were there, so I knew I would be OK.

February

I was chatting with a group of friends including Tamzin Outhwaite when Amanda Holden came over. Amanda is a talented, pretty girl, but she has been quoted in the press as saying some unpleasant things about me in the past. If this was true (which would surprise me) it's all a bit silly because she doesn't even know me – we've hardly even met apart from the occasional time we run into each other at the hair salon or parties within the business. At the wedding she came up and started to talk to me. I really could see no point in chatting to her for too long. She got a bit upset, so I took her away from the rest of the crowd to explain it wasn't a big deal, let's just stay out of each other's way. Despite the press speculation (there's a surprise!) I didn't, and haven't, pinned anyone against a wall. I howled with laughter when I read the article in the press. Not only is it not ladylike, I would never behave like that at someone's wedding. Despite our differences, myself and Amanda are grown-ups and I wish her all the best in the future, and maybe one day we might get to know each other properly.

I didn't stay very late that night as I had a photo shoot for the cover of my book in the morning and I needed to be bright-eyed and bushy-tailed. I got up at the crack of dawn the next day ready to make my way to the Worx Studios, which is tucked around the back of a small mews in Parsons Green, West London. Mum had left early as well but she has to travel on the M11, which is notorious for hold-ups. Today the traffic jam was really bad. Mac encountered problems too, but eventually everyone arrived. My publishers had sent a team along to make a promotional video for the book, so the studio was full of activity.

I had one of my usual teams: Jonathan Malone was doing my hair, Chris Colbeck my make-up and Linzi was doing the styling. It can take a while for hair and make-up to be done, and for outfits to match the backdrop – but ultimately it's worth it. If you get a few shots you're truly happy with, then it's all been worthwhile. Mac took some beautiful shots – one of which was used for the book cover!

At lunchtime that day, Mum took a call from Jaine at my management. I was being offered the female lead in a series of four commercials. It really sounded like fun. Depending on the deal, I agreed in principle. For now, though, I needed to get this book cover done and dusted.

Photo shoots always drag on and today, as usual, we didn't finish when we were supposed to. I was terribly late for my next appointment, and it was another mad rush. Mum set off back to Essex knowing the traffic was going to be bad, but at least we'd had a day together. I needed to get my appointments finished before a nice dinner and an early night as I had another photo shoot the next day.

Getting ready for my photo shoot.

Leaving the studio after the *Telegraph* shoot. I adored that red Dolce & Gabbana coat!

It was yet another early rise for me as I was scheduled to do a photo shoot that Moira Bellas, my publicist, had organised with the *Telegraph*. I was really looking forward to this as it was a special on the BAFTAs and the magazine would be given out at the ceremony. The location was Somerset House and I had my usual team with me. It was one of those months when I'm inundated with interviews and photo shoots. Some are fabulous and others drag on, but I'm happy to be asked so often.

The rest of February was full of meetings with lawyers and accountants. Mum always comes with me to these, and we take a deep breath and get through the day. Rhian Williams, my lawyer at Schillings, ensures our meetings are always OK. We get on well, and she understands me very well nowadays. Laura Holman, my accountant, makes the accounts work more bearable too, and I feel that at last I'm starting to build a good team around me. As for everything else on the work front, things were pretty quiet. I could say that I started to panic as there seemed to be no good-quality work around, but the truth is I really enjoyed my own time. It was great to sit by myself and have time to truly think about what I want from life as well as my work. I've definitely realised that, while work is a great passion, it is just work and isn't *all* of my life any more.

I also loved having the chance to get away with James, to give our relationship the time it deserved before things got manic again. You never know which road your life will take next but in an ideal world I would love to have that happy balance of work and play. As far as work goes, I've done lots of different jobs within the industry – recording, musicals, film, TV, presenting — and I've loved them all. I really like to try different things and I'm proud of everything I've done, especially my *EastEnders* days – they taught me so much and ultimately gave me the career I have today. 'Variety is the spice of life' as they say – and with my work I have to agree.

The location was Somerset House and I had my usual team with me.

Striking a pose for the
paparazzi at the
'Nibbies'.

Valentine's Day was near and I had no idea what would happen. I did know, however, that James was planning something. As the day approached, I was told that I would be picked up from my flat and driven to his house. I spent the day getting my hair done and making myself look as pretty as possible.

On my arrival that night, I went inside. The house was full of flowers and scented candles and it looked beautiful. James greeted me at the door with a wonderful kiss and cuddle before sitting me down to a candlelight dinner, which he'd prepared himself. The food was wonderful. James had gone to a lot of trouble. After dinner we cuddled up to watch some romantic videos and he gave me my presents. As you can imagine, this was a wonderful surprise – and also very private. Therefore I'm sure you'll understand that on this occasion I left the camera in my bag.

This month I was waiting to hear news of my cousin Carrine's baby. She'd been due to give birth in January but had to be induced, and we were all waiting to hear whether the baby had arrived. I was so pleased when I found out she'd had the baby and it was fine – Carrine adores children and she's made a career as a nanny.

So we all descended on Carrine and Howard in their beautiful bungalow. Carrine had been redecorating for ages and had done an amazing job. Although we were really tired after a terrible journey there, we had a wonderful evening. Lewis, the baby, didn't mind being passed round, so everyone had a cuddle. LJ was smitten with him and cradled the little bundle very carefully. Now he wasn't the baby of the family any longer, and he seemed really pleased.

A few days later I had to jet off to Florence to meet an important producer. I was due at the British Book Awards right after I got back but I almost didn't make it as there were big delays on the return flight. But I finally arrived, got myself ready in half an hour and made it – thank goodness. The British Book Awards is an important ceremony dedicated to the book world. Its informal title is the 'Nibbies' because the awards look like golden pen nibs, and everyone involved in book publishing goes along. It's traditional to meet the press first, followed by dinner and then the presentation, and I'd been asked to present the award for Biography of the Year.

William, from my management team, was my escort for the night, and I was seated with my publishers, HarperCollins, and several other people from the book world including the wonderful Michael Palin, Carole Vorderman and Trinny and Susanna, from *What Not To Wear*.

The setting for the event was very lavish. The venue was the Great Room, Grosvenor House, in Park Lane, and the event was strictly black tie. I was in a little chiffon top with tight black flares, my hair was swept back and I wore a pair of fabulous vintage earrings. It was an interesting evening and I got a real insight into the politics of the book publishing business and the people involved. I had a

At the British Book
Awards, with my
publisher Amanda Ridout.

wonderful night and realised just how big these book awards had become.

February is also my nanny's birthday. Nanny Hemmings is a very special lady. I love her madly and she was there to look after me all those years ago when Mum had three jobs at the same time. She would take me to school every morning and collect me afterwards and I would chat with her for hours about anything and everything. I know she's very proud of me now, and I try to see her as often as I can.

Nanny still lives in Hackney and is very independent. After all these years living in England, she still has an Irish accent so strong that hardly anyone can understand her. Her little flat is always immaculate and the kettle is always on. Nanny has a great social life too – I joke to her that whenever I ring she's out!

I like to take Nanny out for her birthday, and this year I decided to take her to Langan's Brasserie in the West End. So I booked the table and ordered a huge bouquet of flowers and a special gift. It would be the first time Nanny had met James, and I wanted her opinion. Mum and Alan picked her up and we all met at the restaurant. Nanny loved James instantly and before long the pair of them were laughing and joking.

It happened that Tom Jones was dining there that night with a friend and his grandson (we've worked together when we've both been guests on TV shows). I went over to say hello to Tom and his companions, thinking that Nanny would enjoy being introduced. Nanny is always game for a laugh and she was really pleased to meet him. 'He looks the same as he always has,' she said, and she was thrilled when he joined in singing 'Happy Birthday' to her later on. It had been a memorable night for Nanny – I'm so glad she enjoyed herself. Mum and Alan took her home and she chatted all the way, saying she would never forget it. Another job well done.

It had certainly been a busy month. I'd secured the TV commercial and now had to go for fittings and meet up with the directors. I also had a photo shoot for *Marie Claire* in aid of the NSPCC. I was absolutely thrilled with the results. Cat Deeley, Denise Van Outen, Billie Piper and myself had all agreed to do a shoot for a charity of our choice and I chose the NSPCC. I've done work for them in the past but it had been a while – it all gives the charity a higher profile and therefore helps them to raise money.

For the cover, I wore an amazing yellow Dior dress that showed off my curves brilliantly and I have to say the photo was one of my all-time favourites. I love *Marie Claire* anyway, especially as when I needed promotion for 'Perfect Moment', and other magazines turned their noses up, they gave me a cover and made me look a million dollars. I was filming the video for the song in New York at the time and they shot the cover out there. I remember feeling pretty unconfident about myself – but the stylist put me in some amazing clothes and before I knew it I felt really special. Now it was my turn to return the favour.

Just after the birth of my nephew, baby Lewis.
We thought it would be very funny if I joined in and put a woolly hat on.
I now realize how stupid I look.

March is always an incredibly busy month for me and it became even busier this year once I decided to give Mum a surprise birthday party. I also had my debut commercial for MFI to shoot. And I was in the studio with Lord Lichfield as well to shoot a poster campaign to tie in with the TV ads. This was the commercial I originally heard about last month, when I was doing the shoot for my book cover. As it was the first fully endorsed commercial I had ever done, I thought about it long and hard before I agreed. I was in good company with several other celebrities who had decided to get involved.

On Wednesday 5 March I set out for the studios to film the commercial. There was a wonderful atmosphere at the studio and I decided it was going to be a great day. Arriving on set at around 8am, I went straight into make-up and saw a newspaper on the table. I was surprised to find that I'd taken up the whole of page three – and the only reason was because of a pair of trainers I was wearing! I'd bought them in Florence and I did think they were the coolest ever – however, the Iraq war was going on and I couldn't believe I was getting such attention in the press for wearing them.

Myself with Neil Fox, who has always been really supportive of my music, my acting and my perfume! He says I'm the best-smelling girl in showbiz, and I always tell him the latest fragrance I'm wearing so he can buy it for his wife – what a gent.

The shoot took a long time to set up, but I had a body double who helped to reduce the waiting around. The commercial was set in an apartment, the type they envisaged I might live in, and I was filmed trying to find my passport as I was supposed to be late for a flight to somewhere like LA. The camera followed my hands as I searched under the sofa cushions (it's the sofa that the ad is all about – essentially the concept of the ad was: who's sofa is this?) Eventually I found the passport and the camera revealed it was me – and my sofa. Before I knew it, the time was 6pm and the ad was a wrap.

The following Tuesday I set out to shoot the poster campaign with Lord Lichfield. I was looking forward to it as I had been delighted with a shoot he had done for me during the promotion of my album for the *Radio Times*. I remember Lord Lichfield had been very sweet on the previous shoot, and he'd done me a huge favour. I'd promised to do a shot for a diabetes charity, wearing denim. He allowed me to change into this quickly and took a fabulous shot that same day, despite his hectic schedule. He has the most amazing stories about the people he's taken photographs of, royalty and stars. He also told me all about the island of Mustique and I ended up agreeing to call him to arrange a trip out there. He's had a house out there for years and we agreed I might stay there. The pictures for the MFI campaign were soon done and we were all very happy.

While I appreciate how hard it is for smokers to quit, I'm an avid non-smoker. I hope I can help people in some small way to overcome their habit, which is why I agreed to help on National No Smoking Day. The campaign is supported by Nicorette, and I was asked to give my help by going down to Capital Radio, supporting the campaign with the press and going on the radio with Dr Fox to chat about it. To be honest, I also saw it as an opportunity to name and shame my mum, who's been a heavy smoker since she was a teenager.

It really is a good cause to support. Thousands of people die unnecessarily due to smoking-related diseases, and there's so much support available nowadays that it's become much easier to try and quit. I was accompanied by William from JJB Creative who'd just given up a forty-cigarette-a-day habit with the help of Nicorette patches. I was very proud of him and I wish him continued success. Linzi had also given up smoking with the help of hypnosis – and Mac managed it by sheer willpower. So now only Mum was left.

I'd been extremely busy that week and Mum's birthday was on Saturday. I'd been quite sneaky and managed to convince her that we were just going out for a family meal. Auntie Kim had helped me with a list of invited guests, and there were seventy people who had accepted and were ready and willing to surprise Mum. She was well and truly in the dark, which was amazing as my family is notorious

The surprise party for my Mum. We'd told her we were going to dinner at Gordon Ramsay's at Claridges and she was getting worried because she'd phoned round and everyone had said they couldn't make it. We had a beautiful suite to get ready in. It had a grand piano so Anthony, my PA, played some of our all-time favourites while we had our hair and nails done. Carl Chapman, who organized the party, did a wonderful job of keeping it hush-hush until the very last minute. Finally we went downstairs and as the doors opened on to a huge room called the French Salon, there were Mum's family and friends all yelling 'Surprise!' Her face positively glowed. I didn't have much time to sort things out for myself but I decided to wear a couture Christian Lacroix dress that I'd only worn once before, to my 21st birthday party. I was delighted to find it was too big now and I had to keep hoisting it up all evening. We had a beautiful dinner, while a fabulous duo who'd flown in from America sang Mum's favourite Motown and blues songs. Then we all got merry and danced the night away. Even Mac joined in! I'll never forget how happy Mum was and I felt so proud that I could do something like that for her.

Jenny's 21st Birthday Celebration
(Again)

Saturday 15th March 2008
Claridge's, London

for being unable to keep secrets. In fact I'd arranged a surprise party at Claridge's but Mum still didn't know. All she knew was that I'd arranged dinner at Gordon Ramsay's restaurant, and Alan was going to bring her down to my suite where a team of stylists would do her hair and make-up as a special treat.

The Thursday before, Linzi, James and me took Mum on a shopping trip to Harrods, saying we wanted to get her something to wear on Saturday. James had agreed to take the day off work to look after us for the day and we all set off for Harrods for a good girly shop. To my amazement, when we pulled up in front of the store there was a parking space free on a meter right outside. Great. But, just as we went to park, Linzi screeched, 'Oh God, I've left my purse at your flat, Martine!' So James turned the car right around, and back we went to retrieve her purse. That's so typical of Linzi. I'd swear she was blonde and dizzy in a previous life!

When we returned to Harrods the parking space had gone (thanks, Linz), so James went off to park while we went in to get a table for lunch before the real shopping started. James insisted on buying lunch and ordered champagne for Mum, which made a wonderful start to her afternoon. The champagne went straight to my head but it left Mum more enthusiastic than ever, and off she trotted with Linzi to the ladies' fashion department.

Mum and Linzi really get on well – Linzi's like a second daughter to her. Most of my friends love Mum, she's open-minded and fair in so many ways. She gives great advice and all my friends feel very comfortable with her. She has a very good heart but she's also totally protective of me, and not many people would dare to cross her. She feels just as protective towards Linzi too, and they really got on from the first moment they met. Along with my other friends, we are all one big happy family. Although Mum's still young, she's experienced most things in life so we can all talk to her and ask her advice, knowing she won't judge us with outdated opinions.

I finally caught up with Mum and Linzi in ladies' fashions. Mum was busy trying on garments in the changing room. She'd let Linzi pick out clothes for her, the sort of thing she would never normally wear. She was getting the star treatment. Now, Mum is the type who loves trousers, although it dumbfounds me every time – she has an amazing pair of long legs but doesn't like to show them. But Linzi and I were determined she was going to show them at her surprise party.

Articles of clothing were going backwards and forwards. Every now and then Mum would appear from behind the curtains looking shy and coy, but still stunning. It was a difficult decision, but in the end Linzi insisted on buying Mum a three-piece black lace outfit that looked incredible and showed off her wonderful legs. At the same time Mum had seen a gold twin-set that she loved, so I bought her that. All in all, she had

top:
Me and my man.

top right:
Mum cutting her birthday
cake.

bottom right:
Julien McDonald and his
partner Akin.

Me and Linzi sing to Blondie's 'Heart of Glass' in Lacroix and Roland Mouret.

a lovely day. Later I took Mum off for a drink – after all, shopping is thirsty work.

As well as shopping, I needed to finalise arrangements with Carl at Claridge's. Mum had tried inviting people for a drink on Saturday, and she'd called me to say how disappointed she was because no one was around and everyone seemed to have other plans. They certainly did have other plans – mine! I'd been on the phone driving Carl mad for the last ten days about who would be eating fish and who would be eating meat, what kind of candles to have and checking and re-checking the arrangements for flowers and music. Carl was an absolute angel the whole time and so calm and organised. Deep in my heart, I knew it was all going to be nothing less than truly amazing.

Alan arrived on Saturday afternoon with Mum and his friend Paul. Paul was coming to the party, but Mum thought Alan was dropping him off somewhere else. We brought Mum up to the suite and ordered her to get showered. Sara Spa, who was there already, told Mum she would do her a manicure and pedicure as a birthday treat, but said she had to dash off afterwards to meet her boyfriend.

Carl arrived later with flowers and a birthday cake. Mum was really pleased but she still didn't guess what was going on. Jonathan Malone was soon also there to do our hair, while his friend Ginny had come along to do our make-up. By this time we were in a bit of a rush as we were due to make our grand entrance at 7.30pm. For a change it was Mum who was running late.

Yet again Carl arrived at the door, this time to take us down to dinner. He explained to Mum that he would have to take her round the back way to the restaurant, through a kitchen, because the press knew I was there and were waiting in the lobby. Mum went along with this – after all, it's par for the course as the press are often hanging around. She was completely hoodwinked. We made our way through the back corridors, my heart thumping. Could I really pull this off? Mum chatted away, talking about the new Jimmy Choo shoes she was wearing for the first time, and then she started to wonder where Alan was. By then I was getting terribly nervous and I'd run out of answers to her never-ending questions. So, ready or not, I shoved her through the door to one big cheer of 'Surprise!'

To Mum's amazement a huge semicircle of friends was standing there to greet her. She was in total shock, but her face was worth all the hard work and effort. This was a night purely for my wonderful mum. The night was young and it held more surprises. My mum had never had a party for herself on this scale. There were hundreds more people who would have loved to come, but I really wanted only Mum's close personal favourites to be there. I hope she was pleased with the list!

Mum made her way around the room. It was the first time in years she'd seen some of the guests and I'd even managed to track down some of her old school

At Mum's party with
Sam, Hayley and Paula.

friends. It took her ages to get round to everyone. Meanwhile the champagne
flowed and the waiters offered out hors d'oeuvres. We had decided to have little
cones filled with fish and chips and they proved very popular, though Mum was so
busy chatting that she missed them!

Mum had assumed that the night's festivities would begin and end with the
reception, so she was shocked when Carl appeared yet again and announced,
'Dinner is served'. The chef had prepared a special meal for everyone, and the
table looked glorious, with a huge chandelier centrepiece surrounded in flowers. In
fact there were seven tables in all, and all of them equally spectacular. The two big
fireplaces, one at either end of the room, were decorated with flowers, too, which
I'd helped arrange. I'd spent most of the day at Claridge's helping the staff, making
sure that everything was perfect for Mum.

At the end of dinner a huge chocolate cake was served and everyone joined in
singing 'Happy Birthday'. The crowd cheered for a speech. Now although Mum
isn't shy at coming forward, she was utterly unprepared. But being the trouper she is,
she stood in front of the mike to thank everyone around the tables, starting with me.

Not many situations can make me cry, but birthdays – and Mum's in particular – are loaded with emotion, and Mum brought tears to my eyes when she thanked me. There's never been any question that we love each other very much but we both made it doubly clear that night. Mum was brilliant – she didn't forget anyone. She was on an emotional high and wanted everyone to know how thrilled she was. Alan had bought her the most beautiful diamond heart necklace, and she had a stack of presents to open later.

Not to be outdone, I jumped at the chance to make a speech for her in return. She sat there, doing very well to hold back the tears, as I spoke of our journey through life together and what she'd done for me as a child, through my teenage years and into womanhood. I decided to finish off by singing 'Somewhere Over The Rainbow' especially for her. I love you, Mum.

As if all this wasn't enough, it was then announced that the disco had started next door. Again, Mum was amazed and made her way into the next room to try and catch up with her guests and have a chat. And there was another surprise in store. I'd arranged for two ice sculptures to be placed on the bar, one male and one female. The barman would pour your chosen drink into the top, and you would receive the drink out of an unprintable part lower down! It was hysterical – everyone wanted to have a go. Mum thoroughly enjoyed taking her turn while Alan looked on.

Ron, the DJ, played some great tunes to get everyone going. James and I started dancing, along with Mum and Alan, and soon everyone was on the floor. Now Julien MacDonald was up and dancing, but Akin, Julien's partner, was superb. He had amazing energy and everyone wanted to dance with him.

I can't thank everyone enough for what turned into the most marvellous night for Mum – and for everyone else, for that matter. Eventually it was late and everyone was tired apart from a few stragglers – including Mum, who went to the bar to continue her celebrations. As another surprise, I presented Mum and Alan with a suite at Claridge's for the night, and arranged for a few of us to stay and have lunch the next day.

James's sister Natalie and her boyfriend Chris had been unable to attend the party on Saturday night as they had been on holiday. When they arrived back on Sunday they joined us for lunch at the hotel. We told them all about the night before, and Natalie and Chris told us about all they'd done on their first skiing holiday. It was a really fun lunch. But all too soon Mum and Alan needed to head home and, quite honestly, I felt exhausted, I hadn't realised just how tired I was. Mum was still on cloud nine, though, so everything had been worthwhile. I saw Mum off with all her gifts and flowers before making my own way home, shattered but very happy. James and I didn't stop smiling all the way.

Me and James in Mauritius. I was there to do a shoot for Elle magazine with Givenchy and Julien MacDonald. We were constantly hounded by the press, but we still enjoyed ourselves. It was also James's 23rd birthday.

I fell in love with him even more on this trip.

I had meetings to attend and I knew I would be drained of energy, but life goes on and now it was back to the real world. There was light at the end of the tunnel though, because I had a work-related holiday in Mauritius with Julien MacDonald to look forward to. It was a shoot for *Elle* magazine in conjunction with Julien and Givenchy, the design house. Givenchy had a new spa within the hotel that we were going to try out, and both of us had been allowed to take our partners. Sounded like a good, fun deal to me! The treatments were marvellous and Julien and I never stopped laughing, even when we were working on photo shoots all day,.

James and I needed to do some last-minute shopping for the Mauritius trip. It was his birthday while we were away and his mum and dad wanted to have a birthday dinner before he left. We went out on Saturday night to a local little Italian

The pool and beach at Le Touessrok.

Julien is about to show us his Olympic water-skiing champion act – gosh, that man is talented!

restaurant in Chelsea where the owners know us and are really fond of us. It was lovely, but Mum and Alan were unable to come over, so we decided to plan something else for when we got back.

The time eventually arrived for us to depart, and I was really excited. This would be a lovely time for James and me to be together, away from the UK and some of the negative press we'd been receiving.

We were both like two little kids when we boarded the plane. We hadn't actually had a proper holiday on our own together. I'd been to Mauritius previously on a magazine shoot and I knew I would find the place even more magical with James there too. It was a long, long flight, but when we arrived at our hotel suite I was sure the trip had been worth it.

I'd brought along lots of wonderful vintage outfits that a fab little shop in Fulham, called Circa, had lent me and I paraded them at dinner in the evenings – I'm such a poser! The hotel swimming pool was beautiful, and James and I found plenty of time to cuddle up and relax. Unfortunately, even all those miles away, I still had to be on my guard because there were four paparazzi following me around – at the beach, on boat trips – you name it – they were there. Most of the shots were exactly the same: Martine dressed in a bikini with James, Martine on her own in a bikini . . . it went on for days. How dull!

One of the highlights of the holiday has to be the water-skiing incident. James and Akin are quite sporty; they'd been playing golf and are quite competitive creatures. So when we were on our little speedboat and neither of them seemed able to pick up the art of water-skiing we thought we would jack it all in and go somewhere else. I think it was giving the boys the hump that they hadn't conquered it. Julien and I, meanwhile, were catching the rays and drinking pina coladas. Julien suddenly said, 'Sod it, I know I'll be crap, but I think I'll give it a go.' The boys laughed, but Julien soon put them in their place. 'Hold on, hold on, I'm not ready yet!' he said in his sing-song Welsh accent. 'Gimme a minute, gimme me a minute.'

We rolled our eyes, thinking he would never let the boat move, let alone manage to get up on the water-skis. Then the boat's engine started – and before I knew it I was looking at the Olympic water-skiing champion. Julien was grinning from ear to ear, laughing out loud with happiness. 'I can do it, I can do it! Look, one hand! I'm good at this, I am!' I was belly laughing, it was so hilarious. And what was even funnier was the look of shock on the boys' faces. Julien, who had genuinely never done it before, was a natural. When he got back on the boat, he kept saying how easy it was. You shouldn't try too hard, he said, that was the key.

While we were out there, I arranged a dinner for two on the balcony of our suite for James's birthday. It was presented very prettily: there were lots of lovely little flowers placed all over the balcony along with little candles. It was a simple night, but really beautiful. I was very sad to say goodbye to Mauritius and the wonderful weather. All of us had a wonderful time and I shall never forget it.

While I was away in Mauritius, I received news from Mum that my good friend Dee had given birth. The baby had been late and Dee was taken in to be induced. She had a really bad time, but was rewarded with a beautiful baby girl called Maisie Belle, who weighed in at 8lb 11oz. Congratulations to Dee and Leroy!

Now you would have thought I'd learnt my lesson with birthday parties, but Alan has a birthday on 13 April and Auntie Kim celebrates hers the day after. James and I had been in Mauritius for his birthday and so we decided to celebrate his too. James's parents Pat and Terry kindly agreed to hold the surprise birthday celebrations at their house, and I went off to organise the cake and presents. I ordered a large chocolate cake shaped like a rose on a huge base of chocolate sponge, with all their names on it. On the big night, the drinks flowed and the thirty or so guests all had a great time. As usual, Mum and Auntie Kim were the first to hit the karaoke machine. God, they're a hard act to follow – not!

Julien and his partner Akin at Spoons restaurant at Le Saint Géran Hotel.

James's birthday dinner on our balcony by the sea. I had sushi, but he managed to get his favourite steak and chips. That's my boy.

Here we are in April and the year covered by my diary has come to an end. I guess it's just been a normal year for me, really: full of highs and lows in both my professional and personal life.

The year so far has been truly brilliant: not only lots of fun and birthdays but also Connor, my agent, has told me it is time to meet the Americans and fly out to LA to discuss work opportunities. I'm really looking forward to it. What it'll involve, to begin with, is meeting up with agents to decide if we want to work together and find some cracking jobs in America. To be honest, Connor mentioned this to me a couple of months ago but I was scared to proceed for two reasons — firstly, there was a huge war going on right then and, secondly, what if no one wanted me out there? But only time will tell and — as usual — I'll give it my best shot.

April

Well, it may be corny to end this sort of book on a happy note – but that's what you're going to get, because that's how I feel!

Here I am in Hollywood – at the Mondrian Hotel in the Hollywood Hills – the weather is beautiful and I've had a brilliant week. I've met up with two agents from the William Morris Agency, who want to sign me up, and I really liked them. They both knew all about my past projects and were very impressed. They'd even been to see me in *My Fair Lady* and gave me a standing ovation at Drury Lane. They seem tough and positive, just what a girl like me needs. Who knows what will come of it, at least I won't look back and wonder what might have been. If nothing comes of it at least I'll know I gave it my best, and more importantly that I had the confidence to do so. But you know what? It's not the be all and end all – it's my birthday today and my man, Mr Tanner, has taken me out to Rodeo Drive, spoilt me rotten and treated me to dinner at the Ivy. Who knows what tomorrow will bring, but today I'm fit and well and happy, happy, happy.